How to Write Successful Essays, Dissertations, and Exams

Chris Mounsey is Professor of English at the University of Winchester. Chris is author of *Christopher Smart: Clown of God*, a biography of the eighteenth-century poet; *Understanding the Poetry of William Blake Through a Dialectic of Contraries*, and many other books and articles.

HOW TO WRITE
Successful Essays, Dissertations, and Exams

SECOND EDITION

CHRIS MOUNSEY

OXFORD
UNIVERSITY PRESS

Great Clarendon Street, Oxford, OX2 6DP,
United Kingdom

Oxford University Press is a department of the University of Oxford.
It furthers the University's objective of excellence in research, scholarship,
and education by publishing worldwide. Oxford is a registered trade mark of
Oxford University Press in the UK and in certain other countries

First published in 2002 as *Essays and Dissertations* in the One Step Ahead series
Second edition 2013

Impression: 1

British Library Cataloguing in Publication Data

Data available

ISBN 978–0–19–967074–1

Printed in Great Britain by

Ashford Colour Press Ltd, Gosport, Hampshire

Contents

FAQs

10% either way of word count: myth or actual?
Page 56

Where on earth do I start?
Page 5

What is the optimum length of a paragraph?
Page 45–46

What citation format should I use?
Page 139

How many points do I need to make a good argument?
Page 46–47

How best to interpret an essay title?
Page 8–9

How should a paper be formatted?
Page 59–60

What should be the balance between primary and secondary sources?
Page 41–47

What is my position? Where is my focus? Where is my goal?
Page 41, 44, 47

How many quotes should be included?
Page 46

What do I do if I can't find any secondary reading to back up a point I think will contribute greatly and will really 'juice up' my essay?
Page 81–103

Should I use 'I'?
Page 42

How much detail should go into an introduction?
Page 41–43

How can I find the best resources for an essay, and are they of a suitable academic standard?
Page 87–96

Is it okay to do research as I write instead of beforehand? A lot of the time I have ideas of what I'd like to say and then read around these while writing, and this then shapes my argument.
Page 109–112

Where do I start with research if it's an unfamiliar subject?
Page 14–39

How many texts should be in a bibliography?
Page 29

What structure is best? Evidence after the point? Evidence then explain at length?
Page 40–49

How do I write a good conclusion without sounding like I'm repeating myself?
Page 47–48

How much does my opinion count alongside those of the scholars and critics I am writing about?
Page 44

What is the best way to introduce new paragraphs and signpost an essay?
Page 44–47

What is the best way to lay out an essay?
Page 58–64

When faced with a mass of essay questions, how do I go about choosing the right one for me?
Page 12

How do I begin; how do I write a plan? Should I just start writing?
Page 35

What is the most constructive way of planning an essay?
Page 40–49 and 109–112

Where on earth do I start?
Page 14

How do I organize my research? How do I know what information to cut and what information to use?
Page 81

Preface to the Second Edition

Much has changed in the methods of gathering information since the first edition of this book came out. In 2001 Google was only three years old and led researchers to few websites carrying information reliable enough to stand up as academic evidence. Now, as well as Google, Bing, and Yahoo, there is a bewildering range of specifically academic websites offering e-books, journals, and primary materials, so much so that today's student might never need to open a book or go into a library. But even if this is so, the method of writing an essay which demonstrates that your opinion about something is valid, by putting together an argument based on relevant and trustworthy evidence, remains the same.

WHO IS THE BOOK FOR?

It has become clear that nowadays more and more students are coming to university ill-equipped in the knowledge of the basic methods for researching and writing essays. This means that the first year of university study can be very difficult, even alienating, and present a student with a huge change in the way they approach their work.

However, there is only one way to write a successful academic essay. This is not to say all essays should be the same. As with football, by playing according to the rules, every game is different.

The book therefore aims to give a graded approach to essay writing for students from A-level up to Master's degree. It will be most appropriate for those studying arts, law, humanities, and social sciences. However, it will also be useful to science students when they have to present information in narrative form.

It lays out a method that can be adapted for most types of assessments: assessed essays, exams, oral presentations, posters, rationales, dissertations, and long essays.

Introduction

Why an essay?

The essay is a piece of writing designed for academic purposes. It is short enough to be read at one sitting. It communicates detailed information about a subject between people who share a common background of knowledge (experts in the field). In the modern academic world it is often called a 'paper' and published in a specialist journal.

A lot of the work you do from A-level to university is assessed in the form of the essay. It is long enough for you to show that you know something about a particular subject. It is short enough that your tutor can mark it conveniently.

But an essay written for the assessment of your academic progress is a strange beast. Where an academic 'paper' is a means of communicating new information to other people who share a common background of knowledge, an essay is a means of communicating information to your tutor about yourself, and how much you know. The essay you write should tell your tutor that you have understood the information that you have been taught, and that you can argue about it. **You do not have to say anything new**. You have to show that you are becoming one of those people who share the common background of knowledge.

In other words, you have to write your essays in a specific way so that they will show you off to the best advantage. This book is intended to tell you how to go about writing academic essays.

How is the information in this book arranged?

Chapters 2–6 lay out the **method for researching and writing essays** for:

- Anyone who has not written an essay before or for a long time
- Confident A-level students who intend to go to university
- First-year undergraduate students
- ALL students who are writing their first essay at the start of a new course

Chapter 7 gives information about:

- **Time management** for busy students

Chapters 8 and 9 give more **detailed information**:

- For those who are becoming confident about essay writing and want to get higher grades
- Second-, third- (and fourth- in Scotland and Ireland) year undergraduate students
- Masters level students

Chapter 10 applies the essay-writing method for:

- All students who have to take **exams**
- Those who are confronted with other forms of assessment, such as oral presentations, posters, and rationales

Chapter 11 applies the essay-writing method for:

- Students who have to research and write a **dissertation** or **long essay**
- Masters level students

Chapter 12 gives ESSENTIAL information for ALL students about **referencing, notes and bibliography**. It's at the end because although it will be the part you refer to most often, it should be the last thing you do.

Some reading routes	Beginner information	Further details
Your first essay	page 5 – 49	page 50 – 73
When an essay counts	page 81 – 115	page 74 – 80
Dissertations	page 129 – 138	
Exams	page 116 – 128	
Quick reference footnotes	page 62 – 65	page 139 – 152

This is an essay

The word 'essay', as we use it today, comes from the French writer Michel de Montaigne, whose *Essais [sic]* were published in 1580. The Elizabethan scholar Francis Bacon (the man who may or may not have written Shakespeare's plays) brought the form into the English language when he published a collection called *Essaies* in 1597. Since Bacon was arguably the founder of modern academic method, it is perhaps no surprise that the essay has become the mainstay of academic communication.

Soon after, Joseph Glanvill gave us the idea that an essay is an incomplete piece of work. In 1665 he wrote *Scepsis scientifica; or confest ignorance, the way to science*, in which he argued that an essay was an 'imperfect offer at a subject'. What Glanvill meant was that when he wrote his essay he wanted readers to remember he did not know absolutely everything about his subject. This is important to remember . When we write an essay we do not have the space or time to put down everything there is to know about the subject, so we must not try to be the fount of all knowledge. We are just giving our opinion about a little bit of our subject.

The word 'essay' also means 'to try' or 'to test'. In this case, the meaning is derived from metal smelting and goes back to biblical times. The molten metal had to be tried or tested in the fire to make sure it was pure enough, or 'true'. This meaning gives us another clue about how to go about writing an essay, since what we must do is test an idea and demonstrate something to be the case. In other words, an essay is like a scientific experiment, or a court case. It should use evidence in support of an idea.

If we join these two thoughts together—that an essay is an opinion about a little bit of a subject, and that by means of evidence it supports an idea—we come to something like a useful definition of the word 'essay'.

An essay is your opinion about a little bit of a subject, in which you use evidence to support your opinion.

What you have just read is an essay. Why?

- It is an opinion.
- It is based on evidence.
- It does not claim to say everything there is to say about essays.

Chapter summary

The purpose of the essay

The undergraduate essay is designed to show that you know about part of a subject area in some depth. It must also show that you can argue your case.

You should bear in mind three important elements of the essay:

Opinion	This is your contribution. You do not have to say anything new, but must argue for a particular viewpoint.
Evidence	This is the result of your research. The evidence you present should lead to the reasons why your opinion is to be believed.
Brevity	An essay is not trying to say everything about a subject. You need to go into depth about just a little bit of the topic under discussion.

Looking at questions

2

When you start a new topic or module, one of the first things you will be given is a list of essay titles and the date by which it must be finished. The first hurdle to jump is choosing which essay to tackle.

We'll start by considering the sort of titles you might come up against, then we'll go on to how to make your choice.

Specific and general essay titles

Essay titles most often come in two types, the **specific** and the **general**. Which sort you get will depend upon your level, your institution and the exam board or person who sets the titles. Both specific and general questions should be answered a similar way, since:

An essay is your opinion about a little bit of a subject, in which you use evidence to support your opinion.

Specific essay titles

Specific questions have a narrow focus and will name people or historical contexts or specific problems. They may have steers attached to them in the form of extra information to guide your essay. A-level questions are usually of this type:

1. One way in which psychologists carry out research is by gathering a great deal of data about one individual. This method is known as the case study.

   Choose one of the core studies listed below and answer the following questions.

Freud (Little Hans)

Thigpen and Cleckley (multiple personality disorder)

Gardner and Gardner (Project Washoe)

(a) Describe how the case study method was used in your chosen study

(b) Using examples, give two strengths and two weaknesses of the case study as used in your chosen study

(c) Suggest one alternative way your study could have been investigated and say how you think this might affect the results

2. How far and in what ways do you see family relationships as a central concern of *The Tempest*? In the course of your answer: show clearly how the play presents family relationships; comment on what the play suggests about family conflicts.

3. Was military superiority the main reason for the expansion of British influence in India in the period c.1757 to c.1785? Explain your answer.

In the first question with steers A, B, and C, sections A and B of the answer are factual (they contain the **evidence**) and section C contains the **opinion**. In part C, you might argue that Freud made a **more** or **less** powerful argument for the Oedipus Complex by studying one case about a neurotic child in detail than he would have done if he had studied many children who showed different degrees of neurosis.

The second question also asks for **evidence** in the first steer, which asks how family relationships are presented, and for **opinion** in the second steer, which asks you to 'comment' about what the play 'suggests'.

The third question asks for **evidence** in the words 'Was military superiority the *main reason*', which suggests there might be other reasons for you to enumerate. It also asks for **opinion** when it demands you 'explain your answer'.

Specific questions set at university level usually will not have the steers to help:

■ To what extent can it be argued that Byron and Keats are second-generation Romantic poets?

- Discuss the importance of the Tizer brand and its role in the development of the marketing mix.
- Explain Harriet Martineau's role in the creation of sociology as a science.

There is little scope in this type of question. You must write about the people and situations mentioned. But none of the examples has a particular answer in mind: there is no right or wrong answer.

- It might be argued **either way** that Byron and/or Keats were or were not second-generation Romantic poets.
- The importance of a brand name and how it functions in the product's marketing mix is open to debate.
- Whether Harriet Martineau can be thought of as a scientific sociologist, or a sociologist at all, is up to you to choose.

There is room for your **opinion** in specific questions, though it must be based on the **evidence** you can find. But you have to decide for yourself what angle you are going to take when answering the question: **you will have to think up the steer for yourself**.

General essay titles

General questions are more usual in universities and work in a different way. They suggest the area you must write about and give you a steer, but they rarely mention specific people or historical contexts, or specific problems. Examples of general questions might be:

- How great was the influence of women on the development of the novel in the eighteenth century?
- To what extent and in what ways do you think that courts influenced Renaissance culture?
- Evaluate the effect of landscape on the expansion of the town.

There is a lot of scope in this type of question, and they seem trickier to answer.

You might think you have to write about:

- every aspect of all eighteenth-century women's influences on the development of the novel;

- the influence of every type of court on Renaissance culture in England, France, and Italy;
- the effects of every different type of landscape on all the towns in the world.

But you do not. **However general the question your answer must be specific.** The difference with general questions is that you get to choose what you are specific about.

Examples

If you wanted to answer about the influence of women on the development of the novel in the eighteenth century you might start by deciding whether you wanted to write about:

- women **writers** or women **readers**.

If you choose women writers you could then narrow things down further and choose to write on, say:

- **one** or **two** women writers.

To answer the question on Renaissance culture you would need to decide whether you were going to write on, say:

- **Royal** courts or **Law** courts;
- in **one** country.

To answer the question on the effects of landscape on urban expansion you might choose, say:

- **one** or **two** towns;
- towns with different environs.

Understanding the question

If the questions look difficult, and you are not sure what they are asking, try making a 'translation' of the question into terms that you *do* understand. To do this:

- Change only the **variables** of the question and keep intact the **terms** that describe the sort of argument you are asked to make.

Examples of translations

You might translate questions like this:

- To what extent can it be argued that Byron and Keats are second-generation Romantic poets?
  Translation: **To what extent can it be argued** that ducks are birds?
- Discuss the importance of the Tizer brand and its role in the development of the marketing mix.
  Translation: **Discuss the importance of** writing good tunes and their **role in the development of** a successful pop group.
- Explain Harriet Martineau's role in the creation of sociology as a science.
  Translation: **Explain** Elvis Presley's **role in the creation of** rock 'n' roll music as an art form.
- To what extent and in what ways do you think that courts influenced Renaissance culture?
  Translation: **To what extent and in what ways do you think that** your mother influenced your character?
- Evaluate the effect of landscape upon the expansion of towns.
  Translation: **Evaluate the effect of** essay writing on the expansion of your knowledge.
- How far did Handel's music evolve **after he moved to** London?
  Translation: **How far** did Wayne Rooney's football **evolve after he moved to** Manchester United ?

From these examples, you can see that the important words are often the least conspicuous ones.

Here, they are:

- 'To what extent can it be argued …'
- 'Discuss the role of …'
- 'Explain …'

- 'To what extent and in what ways ...'
- 'Evaluate ...'
- 'How far ...'

Each **term** requires that you give evidence, and that you give the evidence as part of an argument. The type of argument you have to make is hinted at by the **terms**:

- **'To what extent can it be argued ...'** suggests you should evaluate the strength of the claim that is made in the rest of the question. Here, it may be quite convincingly argued '... that ducks are birds'. On the other hand, it could be argued that since not all birds have webbed feet, there are grounds for believing that ducks are a special type of bird. In the case of Byron or Keats it could be argued that 'to no extent' could they be called second-generation Romantics.

- **'Discuss the role of ...'** suggests that you have to accept the premises of the question, and that you should describe and comment on them. Here, it is taken for granted that pop groups write tunes, and that pop groups try to be popular. There might, however be various different ways of interpreting the importance of a good tune on popularity, and that is what the question is after. You might want to argue that tunes are unimportant in comparison with the style statement made by the group. In the case of the Tizer brand name, you might want to argue that the old-fashioned name is a positive disadvantage in selling the product to young people, but an advantage in selling it to a mature market.

- **'Explain ...'** also suggests that you have to accept the argument that follows. Your explanation will be finding links between the variables of the question. Here, it is taken for granted that Elvis Presley had an influence on rock 'n' roll music, but that you should give reasons why Presley was quite so influential. Likewise, for Harriet Martineau, although you might argue that she was not influential in her time, from a modern feminist viewpoint she has been thought to be influential.

- **'To what extent and in what ways ...'** introduces a tricky question, since its terms can be read either way. You might argue that your mother did not influence your character at all. She influenced your character in no ways and to no extent. Your answer could go through the common misconceptions about mothers' influence on their children. On the other hand you might argue that your mother was the sole influence on your character. She influenced your character to a great extent and in many ways. In the case of the Renaissance law courts, if you argue that they were the mainstay of Italian society, your answer should give your reasons.

- **'Evaluate ...'** requires that you write about the value of the variables in the question. In our example, you might argue that essay writing contracts your knowledge. Essay writing is of no value to your knowledge. Conversely, you might argue that essay writing is the most valuable way of getting to understand the nuances of a subject. You will have to give reasons for your opinion. In terms of physical geography, after you have given your reasons you might also list other ways of understanding the development of towns (perhaps going into one in some detail) and say why it is not so good.

- **'How far ...'** is another way of giving you the opportunity of agreeing or disagreeing with the variables of the question. You might argue that Wayne Rooney's football did not evolve when he moved to Manchester United—his football remained the same. It did not develop very much at all, because he was a great footballer when he played for Everton. You might argue that it changed a lot when he began playing for Manchester United. In the case of Handel's musical development, you might argue that, since he arrived in London and wrote one sort of music and left off writing another sort of music, his music developed considerably, but you might also argue that Handel's music in the operas is identical with that of the oratorios.

Quote and discuss questions

Another type of essay question comes in the form of a quotation followed by the word 'Discuss'. For example:

- 'Francis Bacon wrote Shakespeare's plays.' Discuss.

These questions look hard, but follow the same pattern as the others. The term 'Discuss' gives you the opportunity to agree or disagree with the variables of the question. In our example, you can agree or disagree with the idea that Francis Bacon wrote Shakespeare's plays.

What is common to all these questions?

All these different types of question are written so that you can argue for or against the ideas in the question. But remember your argument is your **opinion**, and it must be based on **evidence**.

Choosing your title

Choosing which essay title to answer is now quite simple. Base your choice on these processes of narrowing down the topic, and translation.

If the questions are **specific**, ask yourself:

■ Which people or situations did I enjoy learning about the most?

Choose the question in which they are mentioned.

If the question is **general**, you may have more questions to choose between. However, you must write about what you are interested in, so go for the general question which best suits the people or situations that caught your interest.

Above all choose the topic you enjoyed the most so you will be motivated to be able to read enough about it to find your evidence. Only when you have enough evidence will you be able to argue an opinion.

Which essay shall I choose?

When you get your list of essay questions at the start of the course or module:

■ Put it away until you've had enough classes to decide which area of the subject matter you are most interested in.

■ Read the required texts for each week.

■ Don't start doing essay work for a couple of weeks.

When you have decided which topic interests you the most, you can start to gather the information necessary to find the evidence on which to base your opinion.

Chapter summary

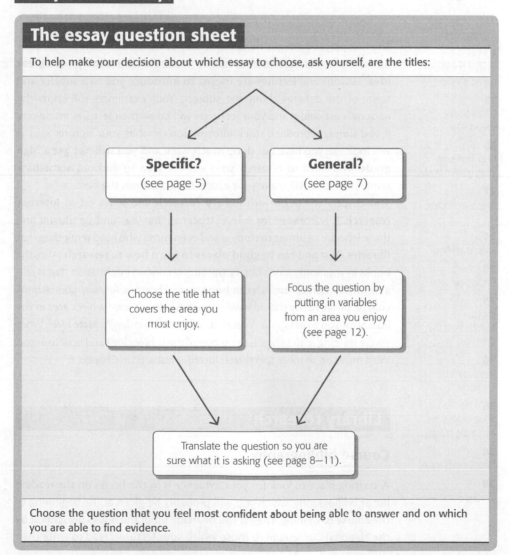

The essay question sheet

To help make your decision about which essay to choose, ask yourself, are the titles:

Specific?
(see page 5)

General?
(see page 7)

Choose the title that covers the area you most enjoy.

Focus the question by putting in variables from an area you enjoy (see page 12).

Translate the question so you are sure what it is asking (see page 8–11).

Choose the question that you feel most confident about being able to answer and on which you are able to find evidence.

3

Research

The first place you might think to look for evidence on which to base your opinion is in your class notes or lecture notes. **This is probably not a great idea**. Lessons and lectures are meant to introduce you to a subject and some of the debates about the subject. Your examiners will know the national curriculum and your lecturers will know their lectures inside out. If you simply reproduce stock information or what your lecturer said, it will look like you have not done much work and **you will not get a high grade**. You need to research your subject area to find out something remarkable that will make your essay stand out from the herd.

This chapter will begin with **library research** and move on to **Internet research**. It is intended for A-level students, first-year undergraduates and those who are returning to study – and even those who need reminding that **libraries exist and can be good places to learn how to research**. Also, the books in your institution's library will largely contain information that is reliable, while Internet research can bring up real horrors. Anyway, your school, college, or university should have enough books on your subject area in the library for you to pass your A-levels and first-year undergraduate level. What you're learning at this stage is the scope of the subject area and how to argue. We'll move on to more specialized Internet research in Chapter 8.

Library research

Course bibliography

A starting place to look for your evidence is in the books on the reading list or bibliography, which you will probably be given at the beginning of the course or module. The list will be made up of the books prescribed by the National Curriculum or those which your lecturers read to write their lectures. When you read these books you will be familiar with the concepts since you will have heard them before in classes and lectures.

More importantly, the bibliography will lead to **other pieces of information** that you can use so it will be apparent that you have done some reading of your own. **This is how to get a higher grade**.

The problem with bibliographies

There is one major problem with bibliographies. Library budgets are small and class sizes are getting bigger, so the books on the bibliography are the first to be checked out. Books need to be circulated among the entire group of students but there are always book hogs who will go to any length to stop books getting around everyone. Remember:

- The best way for books to circulate is to keep them in the library.
  - So try to work in the library.

- If you do check out books, return them promptly when you have finished reading them.
  - You do not have to wait for the return date.

If you follow these ideas, you stand a better chance of seeing the books yourself. Keep mentioning it at your institution's committees, and ask your teachers and lecturers to remind other students to bring books back if there is a queue to read them.

Getting around book hogs

You may be able to get round the problem of book hogs since popular books on a topic (the ones on the bibliography) will often be held in your library on some sort of short-term loan. These will vary:

- Very short loans, where books may not be taken out of the library (four hours is typical);
- For twenty-four hours;
- For a week.

A bibliography is a list of books that were read to find out information on a particular topic.

A note for part-time students

The system of very short loans and twenty-four-hour loans can make it difficult for students who do not have access to the library each day, or for extended periods.

The best thing you can do is to try to work library time into your weekly schedule. Two periods of two hours a week is a good idea.

If you cannot, try to use regular loan books if they are available.

If you cannot manage either of these, you might have to photocopy relevant chapters from the short-loan items. Remember, though, that you can only copy up to 10% of a book without breaking copyright.

Student reserve collections

There may be a student reserve collection for the very short-loan books, so find out if there is and where it is.

- Books might be held behind the main issue desk, and you have to ask for them by title.
- There might be a dedicated room in the library where all the short-loan books are kept, with its own issue and return desk.

When you get your first bibliography, ask your teacher or lecturer if there is a system of this kind, and if there is, go to the library and ask how it works.

You never look stupid asking questions about how to find library books.

Astronomically high fines for late return of short-loan books are usual, so be sure to get them back on time.

Reserving books

If a book is out on short or long-term loan you can usually reserve it so you get to read it next.

- Go to the issue desk and ask about the procedure.

You may even be able to recall it from the person who has it: another good way to get around book hogs.

The problem with short-loan books

Short loans are all well and good, but the system might fail you: either because the books on the bibliography do not quite match the essay you have chosen, or because there is a long queue for the book you think will help most.

DO NOT DESPAIR.

You can always find relevant books that are not on the bibliography.

Finding books on the right topic

Finding other books on a particular topic is not as hard as you might think. There are four methods I shall describe here:

- Shelf mark search;
- Keyword search;
- Author search;
- Bibliography search.

Shelf mark search

This type of search uses the number you find on the back of the book, which the library uses to catalogue it, and to get it on the right shelf so it can be found easily. Most libraries use the Dewey cataloguing system and store books with others on the same or similar topics.

1. Look up the shelf mark of the book on your bibliography that most nearly matches what you want to write about.
2. Write it down.
3. Find the place on the shelf where the book ought to be.
4. Look around on the shelves and you'll find ten, twenty, a hundred, possibly a thousand books on similar topics.
5. Look at the titles on the spines of the books and make your selection.

Keyword search

Another way to find books on your topic, in your library catalogue, is to do a KEYWORD SEARCH.

This sort of search is particularly useful if you are working with a topic that has distinctive words in it.

1. Think up two or three words that might appear in the title of a book that will help you.
2. Write them down.
3. Enter the words in your library computer Keyword Search function.
4. Your bibliography will appear.

Example

You are writing an essay on the Renaissance courts.

1. Choose the words 'Renaissance' and 'courts'.
2. Enter them on your library computer Keyword Search.

On my library computer, titles of twenty books appeared.

The problem with keyword searches

Where your subject is less specific, you might find you get a very long list of titles.

A keyword search on 'physical' and 'geography' produced 436 books on my library catalogue. If this happens, try adding a third keyword. In the example, of 'physical' and 'geography':

- Adding the word 'British' gives seven books.
- Adding the word 'sea' gives twenty books.

The third word you choose will narrow down the field. Your choice of which word depends on your topic.

Author search

On your library's catalogue, select the function AUTHOR SEARCH. If someone has published a book on a topic, they often publish another.

1. Enter the name of an author from the module bibliography.
2. Note the shelf mark of any other books the author has written, and find the book.

This search method will produce only a few books. However, you can use just one book on a subject to find many more. You can do this by using a BIBLIOGRAPHY SEARCH.

Bibliography search

Find any book on a subject close to that of your essay (perhaps one you have found in the author search). Turn to the back and you will almost certainly find a BIBLIOGRAPHY. It may be called a (LIST of) WORKS CITED. For example, in a book on Handel, a few entries are:

Bibliography
Gentry, Peter W. *Methodism and Messiah: Reflections on John and Charles Wesley, the early Methodists and George Frederic Handel's great oratorio.* Sheffield: Wesley Fellowship, 2011.
Greene, David B. *The theology of Handel's 'Messiah', Beethoven's 'Credo', and Verdi's 'Dies Irae'.* Lewiston, NY: Edwin Mellen Press, 2012.
Leon, Donna. *Handel's Bestiary: In search of Animals in Handel's Operas.* London: Heinemann, 2011.
Vickers, David, ed. *Handel.* Farnham: Ashgate, 2011.

This is the list of books the author read to research for the book. These books will therefore be relevant to your topic as well. Check if you have any of them in your library.

Which books should I use?

There are two basic guidelines you should bear in mind when collecting evidence for writing A-level essays and for first-year degree essays:

First: if the book is not held at your library, do not look for it elsewhere.

- Your institution ought to hold all the books necessary for passing your course.
- Unless you are going to refer to it more than once, buying a book may not be worth it (except when you really like the subject).

Second: if the book is over ten years old, think twice about using it. The ideas could be out of date.

Some books have become classics in their field, but you will know a book like this is all right to use since it will have been republished and will therefore have a publication date that is less than ten years old.

Finding the relevant information in books

After all these different searches you should have a fair quantity of books on your library table.

- Open the first book on your pile.

Start with the **contents page** where the chapter titles are given.

Read them over and decide if one or two seem as though they are relevant to your essay.

If they are:

- Note down the title of the book and the chapter number and title.

If not, turn to the back of the book and look up some relevant words in the **index**.

- Look for ranges of pages cited (that is over two pages) and ignore single-page citations.

If there are none, or only a few references, put the book aside.

Move on to the next book and repeat the process until you have gone through the whole pile of books.

Your own reading list

You should now have two piles of books, the ones with relevant chapters or passages and the ones that have nothing interesting for your essay. You should also have a list of relevant chapters or passages in the relevant books.

Take the reject pile of books to the re-shelving trolley so that other people can get a look at them in case the books are relevant to their essay. **Remember, there will be a whole group of you working on the same essay at the same time**. Don't be a book hog.

The other books will have one or more chapters or passages that seem relevant to your essay, and you will have a list of these extracts since you will not be 2able to read them all at one sitting.

Internet research

Another way to find information for an academic essay is by using the Internet. At this stage we'll look at some basic ways to search for information that is reliable to use as evidence in an academic essay. Later in the book (Chapter 8) we'll revisit Internet research and look at it in more detail.

The most important thing to remember about information that you find on the Internet is that **most of it is very low-level** and can be used sparingly at A-level, but certainly not for degree essays. A rule of thumb is that if whole books or academic articles, which are still in copyright (that is, 90 years after the author's death), are available for free, then they are not worth using. They are either illegal copies, and downloading them can incur a huge fine, or the information has not been checked for quality and so is not valid for academic use.

Two Unbreakable Rules of Internet searching

- Never cut and paste paragraphs from the Internet directly into your essay.
  - Treat the Internet as the beginning, not the end, of your research.

In the academic world, a piece of information is only valid if it has been 'double blind' peer reviewed.

21

- ■ ALWAYS CHECK EVERY PIECE OF INFORMATION YOU FIND.
  - – Find out where the idea came from.

But there are exceptions, and Internet searching can prove very fruitful.

Narrowing down your search results

If it is daunting to find a list of 436 books on your library catalogue when searching for books on Physical Geography, a return of 5,120,000 items on the same search with an **Internet search engine** such as Google, Bing, or Yahoo can seem like far too much information. But there are ways of finding reliable and relevant information and avoiding the major pitfalls of Internet research.

In this section we will look only at Google, the most widely used free-access search engine.

When you type in your search 'Physical Geography', Google will give you options to narrow your search before you click the search button – when I did the search, this appeared:

- ■ of Greece
- ■ of India
- ■ of China

Take the initiative from this list and put in, for example, 'of Britain'. Google now changes its options list to:

- ■ Physical geography of Great Britain
- ■ Physical and human geography of Great Britain
- ■ Physical geography of Great Britain and Northern Ireland

TIP: If you are searching Google for an exact phrase, put the phrase in double quotation marks and Google will return only hits in which it appears.

Once again you can take the initiative and narrow down your search further with different terms, or you might choose to click one of the options.

Sifting your results

You might think you can use any of the results you find that look relevant to your essay **but this is where you have to be most careful**. If the information on a website is surrounded by advertisements, links to quizzes or to things that are not relevant to your topic, then the website is more interested in selling than informing.

Be careful, some websites disguise their adverts in neat lists that look like the information—they are still adverts and the site is selling, not informing. Sites like these are only good for GCSE.

Wikipedia

This site will be the first result on nearly all your searches.

ALL teachers and lecturers will tell you:

- It is unreliable.
- It should NEVER be cited.

But used with circumspection, it can point your research in the right direction.

Because the site can be edited, unscrupulous people alter the information on it, simply for badness. So follow the **two Unbreakable Rules of Internet research**:

- Never cut and paste paragraphs from the Internet directly into your essay.
- ALWAYS CHECK EVERY PIECE OF INFORMATION YOU FIND. This goes for Wikipedia too. The articles tend to be cut-down versions of more scholarly articles.

So:

- Read the Wikipedia article to get a general understanding of your topic.
- At the bottom of the article and you'll find a list of books and other materials in the sections marked:
  - References
  - Bibliography

These will give you the list of information sources and books the writer of the article read, so they will be relevant, and above all they are useable in an academic essay.

BUT BEWARE

If the information is web-based, go to the website and CHECK IT.

- Websites are sometimes bogus:
  –e.g. Most websites about the novelist Bret Easton Ellis are an elaborate joke.

- Websites go out of date or are replaced:
  –e.g. Government websites are constantly being replaced or rebuilt.

All the websites listed on our example of the Physical Geography of Britain search that leads us to the Wikipedia entry 'Geography of the United Kingdom' (accessed 3 August 2012) have been superseded by new UK government websites from the Office of National Statistics (⬏ <http://www.ons.gov.uk>). Likewise, the one book cited is dated 2000, so it is also out of date.

THIS IS NOT ALWAYS THE CASE

The Wikipedia entry for **Harriet Martineau** is much more heuristic. It offers:

- A bibliography of books she wrote;
- A bibliography of books about her;
- A list of references to relevant sources.

This is a gold mine of information—BUT IT IS UP TO YOU TO GO AND FIND IT.

The Wikipedia bibliography of books by Harriet Martineau lists three like this:

- *The Hour and the Man: An Historical Romance*. 1839, Project Gutenberg
- *The Crofton Boys: A Tale*. Charles Knight, 1841, Project Gutenberg
- *Household Education*. 1848, Project Gutenberg

Free Internet sources

Project Gutenberg is a volunteer organization, set up in 1971, which digitizes books that are out of copyright and makes them available in a variety of formats.

- If a book is listed on Wikipedia as Project Gutenberg, click the Project Gutenberg icon and you will be taken directly to the book.
- If it is not, search the Project Gutenberg site (◪ <http://www.gutenberg.org>).

Another site that leads you to many more free books is The Internet Archive (◪ <http://www.archive.org>).

- This site has 183 versions of books written by Harriet Martineau.
- All of them can be downloaded free and legally.

Books can be read online or downloaded in a variety of formats:

- PDF
- Epub
- Kindle
- Daisy

BUT all these books are out of copyright, so will be primary sources (books written by the focus of your research), not secondary sources (books written about the focus of your research),

AND YOU NEED BOTH.

The Wikipedia bibliography of books about Harriet Martineau lists three:

- David, Deirdre. *Intellectual Women and Victorian Patriarchy: Harriet Martineau, Elizabeth Barrett Browning, George Eliot.* Ithaca: Cornell University Press, 1989. ISBN 0-8014-9414-1
- Logan, Deborah Anna. *The Hour and the Woman: Harriet Martineau's "Somewhat Remarkable" Life.* DeKalb, IL: Northern Illinois University Press, 2002. ISBN 0-87580-297-4
- Sanders, Valerie. *Reason Over Passion: Harriet Martineau and the Victorian Novel.* New York: St. Martin's Press, 1986. ISBN 0-7108-1018-0

Of these three, only the second is (just) possible to use. The others are out of date.

BUT help is at hand!

1. Copy the title of one of the books – say the first one.
2. Paste it into the Google search box.
3. Click 'Books' on the left side of the Google screen. More than 1,500 results appear on Google Books.
   - Not all these results are books about Harriet Martineau.
   - BUT they are all relevant to her.
   - Read the brief description in black. It will tell you enough to know if it is in the right area for your essay.
   - HOWEVER, they may not all be useable. Check the grey writing after the name of the author.
     - Deirdre David's book has a 'Snippet View'.
     - There may be a few quotes available from the book, but nothing substantial.
     - BUT the next book in the search, *Women Constructing Men* by Sarah Frantz and Katharina Reinhak (2010), has a 'preview'.
     - FIVE other books on the first page also have previews.
       - The publisher has licensed Google Books to show some parts of the book.
       - This means that a number of the chapters will be available for you to read online.

THESE BOOKS MAY BE IN DATE (**CHECK**) BUT:

- THEY ARE NOT WHOLE BOOKS
- YOU CANNOT DOWNLOAD OR COPY FROM PREVIEWS
- PAGES OF CHAPTERS MAY BE MISSING

Click the title to read the preview on screen.

In the bar on the left-hand side of the reading pane, you can:

- SEARCH inside the preview of the book *Women Constructing Men*.
- A search on 'Martineau' leads you to a chapter by Frederick Burwick and other page references.

- You will also be prompted to:
    - −BUY the eBook
    - −BUY the book in print

You might, however, find the book in your institution's library.

Journal databases

The Internet searches we have done so far have all been free. Universities also pay for access for you to a number of databases of academic journals. We'll look at just one here called JSTOR, because it encompasses a wide range of topics. The JSTOR database lets you perform a **basic search**, which is good for:

- Topics
- Names
- Specifics of any kind

But if you are researching for a **general question**, and you are not sure which specifics you want to argue, you can begin with an **advanced search**. Let's start with another of the questions from the last chapter:

- How great was the influence of women on the development of the novel in the eighteenth century?

Because this is a general question, you do not have a name or specific to look up in the question, so open the 'Search' menu and choose 'Advanced'.

JSTOR gives you two search boxes, each of which has search options within:

- Full-text
- Author
- Item title
- Abstract
- Caption

You can also add any number of search boxes by clicking 'Add a Field'.

For the example, we shall search using **three words taken from the question**:

> **Women (in 'Full-text')**
> **Novel (in 'Item title')**
> **Eighteenth (in 'Full-text')**

So add one field and type each word in a separate box, changing the search option for 'Novel'.

Below the search boxes you can also narrow down your search to papers published with the acceptable date range of ten years. This search garners 159 results (accessed 3 August 2012).

Not everything will be relevant, but with a list of this length you should go through it all.

There are two types of entry:

JOURNAL ARTICLES—for example:

O'Brien, Karen. 'History and the Novel in Eighteenth-Century Britain'. *Huntington Library Quarterly* Vol. 68. No. 1–2 (March 2005), pp.397–413.

- Click the title and you will be taken to the abstract.
  - This is a brief account of what is in the article.
- Read it, and if it looks relevant:
  - Download the whole article as a PDF.

REVIEWS—for example:

David Wayne Thomas. Review of *Consensual Fictions: Women, Liberalism and the English Novel* by Wendy S. Jones. *Victorian Studies*, Vol. 48, No. 4 (Summer 2006), pp.762–4.

- Click the title and you will be taken to the review.
- Read it, and if it looks relevant:
  - Go to Google Books to see if there's a preview of Wendy Jones's book, OR
  - Go to your library and see if there is a copy.

How many books or articles is enough for an essay?

- You will know when you have enough material because your reading will begin to give you a feel for what you are going to argue.
- Some people stop after finding one article.
- Some people cannot stop.
- BOTH are wrong. Find a happy medium.

A note on taking quotes

You are now ready to start your research. Whether you prefer to work with paper and pencil or on a laptop, whether you are working from a pile of books or from a list of PDF files, make your life easy. Always note down the full title of the source (book or article) before you copy down a quote.

- Use a new piece of paper for each book or journal article you check through.
- Use a new computer file for each book or journal article you check through.
- When you find a quote make sure you write down the page number too.

Finding quotes

When you start reading either a book or journal article, remember that not everything in the chapter or article will be relevant to your essay. What you are trying to find is evidence from which you can form and support an opinion. When you find an important piece of information, copy down the sentence in which you find it verbatim (that is, word for word) together with the number of the page.

The process is not difficult. But a perplexing question will keep coming up in your head—what is important?

What is important?

The answer to the question is not as hard as it seems.

THE IMPORTANT BITS OF INFORMATION ARE THOSE THAT CATCH YOUR EYE

You are not reading to find a standard set of facts or figures that are necessary for every essay on your topic. Important bits of information are important because they are interesting to you. If they interest you, you will already have formed an opinion about them (that they are interesting) and they will therefore be relevant to your argument.

This means that if you don't know exactly what you are going to write about, take down anything that looks interesting to you. Note down the sentences or paragraphs that contain the interesting bits, and when you have finished reading you will have found out what you are going to have an opinion about.

It will be on the page of notes or in the computer file you have just created.

Example of finding quotes for essays

You are researching, say, an essay entitled: 'How far did Handel's music evolve during his time in London?'

> A question in the **general style** might be: 'How far can England be thought of as sustaining musical evolution in the eighteenth century?' You choose to write about London and Handel's music in particular.

The book you have found that seems relevant is Donald Burrows's *Handel: The Master Musicians*, 2nd edn (Oxford: OUP 2012).

- It is available as a preview on Google Books.
- It is available in paperback, hardback, and on Kindle.
- You have chosen to read Chapter 11, 'The Oratorio Composer I: Dublin and London, 1741–5'.

BECAUSE

- It is about the first performances of *The Messiah*.
- You heard in a lecture that Handel changed his musical style when he popularized a new English form of music, the oratorio.

While you are reading, you discover the first part of the chapter considers the performances of *Messiah* in Dublin.

- It is not relevant to your essay title about London or England.
- YOU TAKE NO NOTES.

The chapter moves to London, though you find nothing interesting, but then something catches your eye and you begin to read carefully.

> It seems quite likely that the coldness between Handel and the Prince of Wales was the aftermath of Handel's refusal to compose for the opera company.[75] Mrs Delany also noted that
>
>> They say Samson is to be next Friday: for Semele has a strong party against it, viz. The fine ladies, petit maitres, and ignoramus's. All the opera people are enraged at Handel, but Lady Cobham, Lady Westmorland, and Lady Chesterfield never fail it.[76]
>
> According to rumours that had reached Lord Shaftesbury before the beginning of the season, the opera supporters even tried to undermine Handel's nontheatre income:[77]
>
>> The Opera people take incredible pains to hurt him. It is said (and I believe true) but why Handel is shy of owning it I cant well guess, I had it from very good hands, that last Saturday the two hundred pounds a year additional to Queen Anne's pension (for teaching the princesses) was taken away from Handel, and that he and several others are turn'd out. He has poor man very powerful enemies.
>
> The number of teachable Princesses in London had diminished during the last decade, but it is uncertain whether Handel did actually lose his post. If Handel's social position in London was not entirely secure, then his decision to open his

---

[75] The dispute between the King and the Prince of Wales (see chapter 9, n.7) was formally resolved following the fall of Robert Walpole in 1742, but Handel's relationship with the Prince in the following years was no doubt affected by the composer's rejection of approaches from the 'opera party'. In 1743 and 1745 the Prince attended the Middlesex opera performances and Handel's oratorios, but in 1744 he attended only the opera. See Taylor, 'Handel and Frederick, Prince of Wales', p.91.

[76] Letter to Mrs Dewes, 21 February 1744: D, p.584.

[77] Letter, Lord Shaftesbury to James Harris, 12 January 1744: B&D, pp.182-3.

season with *Semele* was a brave or possibly foolhardy, gesture. Quite apart from the work's pseudo-operatic manner, the secular story was a peculiar choice for a theatre programme that began on the first Friday of Lent; as Mrs Delany said, her clerical husband did 'not think it proper for him to go … it being a profane story'. But the performances seem to have been well received.

For his cast, Handel retained Beard, Avolio and Reinhold from the previous season, welcomed back Francesina and had two new singers in the contralto Esther Young and the alto Daniel Sullivan. Mrs Delany was not entirely flattering about the singers, after attending the fifth performance:

> I was last night to hear Samson. Francesina sings most of Mrs. Cibber's part and some of Mrs. Clive's: upon the whole it went off very well, but not better than last year. Joseph, I believe will be next Friday, but Handel is mightily out of humour about it, for Sullivan, who is to sing Joseph *is a block* with a very fine voice, and Beard *has no voice at all.* The part which Francesina is to have (of Joseph's wife) will not admit of much variety; but I hope it will be well received; the houses have not been crowded, but are pretty full every night.

'Not crowded but pretty full every night' probably sums up Handel's degree of success in his 1744 season. Mrs Delany supplies the end of the story:

> The oratorios fill very well, not withstanding the spite of the opera party: nine of the twelve are over. Joseph is to be performed (I hope) once more, then Saul, and then Messiah finishes; as they have taken very well, I fancy Handel will have a second sub-scription; and how do you think *I have lately been employed?* Why, I have made a drama for an oratorio out of Milton's Paradise Lost, to give Mr. Handel to compose to.

Handel did not take up Mrs Delany's libretto (though he accepted an invitation to dinner on 3 April), nor did he proceed beyond the 12 performances, which con-cluded on the Wednesday of Holy Week. The last performance was *Saul*, not *Messiah*. Handel was perhaps not yet ready to test out the state of his relationship with London's pressure groups (and Jennens) over that work. His programme had comprised the new works *Semele* and *Joseph* (four performances of each) and revivals of *Samson* and *Saul* (two performances of each).

Joseph and his Brethren has been adversely criticized in modern times for both its literary style and the structure of its libretto, but Handel seems to have had a better opinion of the work and revived it fairly often. *Semele* on the other hand, was not

---

[78] Letter to Mrs Dewes, 21 February 1744: D, p.584.

[79] Handel had also hoped to employ Mrs Cibber for the season: see Lady Shaftesbury's letter of 31 [October] 1743: B&D, p.175.

[80] Letter to Mrs Dewes, 25 February 1744: D, p.585.

[81] Letter to Mrs Dewes, 10 March 1744: D, pp.587-8. In the Autumn of 1744 Jennens was also working on a libretto based on Paradise Lost: see Lord Shaftesbury's Letter, 14 September 1744 (B&D, p.198).

heard after 1744, mainly because Handel abandoned using such secular works as a basis for his programmes. There is no reason to suppose that he found James Miller, the Librettist for *Joseph*, an uncongenial or incompetent collaborator, and Miller for his part gave Handel the strongest support (by implication, against the 'opera' party) in the dedicatory preface to the Duke of Montagu that was printed in the word-book:

> 'Tis a pity however, My Lord, that such a Genius should be put to the Drudgery of hammering for Fire where there is no Flint, and of giving a Sentiment to the Poet's Metre before he can give one to his own Melody.

Unfortunately, their collaboration was curtailed by Miller's death on 27 April 1744. Handel took almost immediate action to secure his future librettos by patching up his differences with Jennens:[82]

> Handel promis'd to revise the Oratorio of Messiah, & he & I are very good Friends again. The reason is he has lately lost his poet Miller, & wants to set me at work for him again.

Handel's performances in 1743 and 1744, presented as Lenten 'oratorio seasons', had established a new pattern for his professional career (the terminological confusion over 'oratorio seasons' is discussed in chapters 9 and 13). With two sufficiently successful seasons behind him, Handel now took the logical, but still surprising step of expanding into a much more ambitious programme: instead of the well-tried base of 12 performances, he planned for a full scale season of twice that length. At 24 performances, this was still only about half the number that had been conventional for opera seasons, but it represented a considerable speculative challenge in relation to the London audience. The immediate stimulant to Handel's scheme was the collapse of the Middlesex opera company: Handel determined to move back to the King's Theatre Haymarket, and offer his own programme of English works 'after the manner of an Oratorio', as a substitute for operas. It was perhaps the one aggressive competitive gesture of his career: he wanted those who had undertaken to 'middle with harmony' not merely to be beaten but to be seen to be beaten.

Note-taking to develop your opinion

What catches your eye was the phrase 'coldness between Handel and the Prince of Wales'. It reminds you of a film you saw, called *The Great Handel* (1942), about Handel writing the *Messiah*. You remember the film showed how partisan people were about music in the eighteenth century. The film showed that Prince Frederick and his friends were in favour of opera, and the king (George II) preferred oratorio.

---

[82] Letter from Jennens to Holdsworth, 7 May 1744: HHB, p.376.

- So you note:

  p.365 It seemed quite likely that the coldness between Handel
  and the Prince of Wales was the aftermath of Handel's refusal to
  compose for the opera company.

The quotes from Mrs Delany and Lord Shaftesbury demonstrate the partisanship of the musical public, but they do not explain 'in what ways or to
what extent Handel's music evolve[d] while he was in London'.

- So you take no notes.

Nor do you need to know about performances of a secular piece in Lent,
nor the cast, nor what Mrs Delany thought of it.

- So you take no notes.

However, the third quote from Mrs Delany mentions oratorios.

- So you note:

  p.366 The oratorios fill very well, not withstanding the spite of
  the opera party: nine of the twelve are over. Joseph is to be
  performed (I hope) once more, then Saul, and then Messiah
  finishes; [Mrs Delany: Letter to Mrs Dewes, 10 March 1744: D,
  pp.587–8.]

Mrs Delany might be interesting (see Chapter 9), but for the present purpose you do not need to know about her libretto, nor about the oratorio
Joseph in modern times. However, the same paragraph tells you:

p.366 Semele on the other hand, was not heard after 1744, mainly
because Handel abandoned using such secular works as a basis for his
programmes.

The word 'abandoned' suggests a change in Handel's musical output.

After some irrelevant information about Handel's librettists, we get
some direct information about his move from secular (opera) to religious
music (oratorio):

- So you note:

  pp.367–8 Handel's performances in 1743 and 1744, presented as
  Lenten 'oratorio seasons', had established a new pattern for his
  professional career ... [which] At 24 performances ... was still only

about half the number that had been conventional for opera seasons, but it represented a considerable speculative challenge in relation to the London audience.

Forming your opinion from the evidence

Beginning with **evidence** from the fourth quote, you can develop an **opinion** that Handel's music evolved *comprehensively* and *successfully* while he was in London.

- The 'Lenten "oratorio seasons", had established a new pattern for his professional career ...'

You can nuance your **opinion** that the shift from secular music to sacred music was not popular with everyone with **evidence** from the first quote:

- '... the coldness between Handel and the Prince of Wales was the aftermath of Handel's refusal to compose for the opera company.'

And you can give weight to your **opinion** that Handel's choice to make the change became *successful* with **evidence** from the second quote:

- 'The oratorios fill very well, not withstanding the spite of the opera party ...'

Finally, you can conclude your **opinion** that Handel's musical evolution was *comprehensive* with **evidence** from the third quote:

- '*Semele* [a secular oratorio] ... was not heard after 1744, mainly because Handel abandoned using such secular works as a basis for his programmes.'

It might seem that you can start to write your essay based upon the opinion gained from this piece of research, but then you would be copying Donald Burrows's opinion, which might not be universally acknowledged.

Evidence from the **other books and journal articles** you will read to research for this essay may alter or nuance your opinion, and **that** is the value of researching from more than one source.

Developing the argument

An important difference in essay writing between undergraduate level and A-level or Access course is that at the higher level you are graded more on your ability to make a **coherent argument**, and less on the amount of information presented.

The way to think about it is to remember that in all the A-level and Access course essays you have to say a little bit about a lot of information.

In an academic essay, you need to say a lot about a little bit of information.

- Do not write a long list of facts about your topic. You have to say something interesting about five or six facts.

To do this, you have to focus in on the facts in great detail, so that you can arrange the facts into an argument.

Ask yourself: What am I trying to argue?

This is where you can go back to your translation of the question. For example, you might 'translate' the following essay question:

- How great was the influence of women on the development of the novel in the eighteenth century?

into, say:

- How great was the influence of my favourite singer on the music of the early twenty-first century?

Now let us explore the different ways you can argue.

Types of argument

When you have decided what the question is asking, and you have done your research, write out a brief answer in about 100 words.

An answer to the example question in its translated form might go something like:

> I think my favourite singer contributed greatly to recent developments in music. I would emphasize three key points. First, her songs have been re-recorded by more than twenty other popular musicians; second, her music is to be heard daily on the radio; third, her tours sell out hours after they are announced. Having said that, however, I think that it is fair to say that the second and third points are also applicable to several other singers and pop bands who have one hit song that is quickly forgotten. So all things considered, I think it might be best to argue that my favourite singer's influence was limited to just the first of my original three points.

Another answer to the same question, which would lead from different evidence, might be:

> My favourite singer played no part in the recent developments in music. Latest research shows that popular music is entirely conditioned by the colour of shirts young people wear, and not by listening to the music made by other musicians. This has been shown to be the case by Professor Joao Bloggs in the book Shirt colour and the writing of pop songs. Of course I, like everyone else, instinctively feel that other contemporary music does influence developments in the form. But the scientific evidence to the contrary compels me to conclude that this feeling is misleading, and that shirt colour alone is the influence on contemporary popular musicians.

- ▪ What makes these answers good is that they are made up from coherent arguments, and based on acceptable evidence.
- ▪ Degree essays are not looking for a right or wrong answer, but a good argument either way.

By contrast, the following is a bad answer to the same question.

> In order to answer the question, I shall tell you something about my favourite singer. She is Canadian, born of Caucasian and native American parents. She began to write songs while at school in Michigan, and played in folk clubs while she was at university. At one club in Chicago she was heard by a talent scout who signed her up to A&B records. The main influences on her music were native American music, jazz and folk music, and we can hear these three strands clearly throughout her oeuvre. Her most commercially successful album was Music is the colour of my shirt, which sold 5 million copies. Thus we can be sure that her music influenced many musicians of the early twenty-first century.

What makes the bad answer unsatisfactory is not that the facts are wrong—there are lots of them, and they are presumably correct—but that the conclusion does not lead from the evidence, and so there is no coherent argument.

The facts about the musician's life, even the popularity of one album, do not demonstrate an influence on any other musicians. The facts may be correct but they are irrelevant to the question.

What should I argue?

There is no right answer that will guarantee you high marks. You will be graded on the **coherence** of your argument, not on whether you agree with the examiner.

But however coherent your argument, your essay will not work if it is not easy to read. There are two elements to making your essay an easy read: the structure of the essay, and the clarity of your language. These topics will be covered in Chapters 4 and 5.

Chapter summary

The process of research

Remember that research is not a search for a particular set of facts. Any fact you find interesting will probably be useful for your essay.

Find books

- Bibliography search
  - Are the books on ordinary loan?
  - Are the books on short loan?
- Shelf mark search
  - Are there any other books with the same shelf mark?
- Keyword search
  - A library computer search
  - One/ two/ three keywords
- Author search
  - Find a book by the author of another on your bibliography, and check its bibliography
- Internet search
  - <http://www.google.com>

Use these methods to create your own reading list.

Take quotes

Quotes you might use in your essay will be those sentences you read that catch your eye.
  When you take a quote, note down the details of the book you found it in:

- Author's name;
- Title of the book;
- Publication details (place: publisher, date);
- Page number.

Form your opinion

Use the quotes and notes as evidence on which to base your opinion. What does the evidence suggest to you?

4 Structuring the essay

The decision about what information goes where in an essay can be complicated. Based on what you have learned so far, you can make these decisions much more easily.

1. You are writing an essay in order to give your **opinion** about something, so first:
   - Introduce your opinion and your reasons for holding it.
2. You must offer **evidence** as to why your opinion is valid, so next:
   - Present evidence for your opinion.
3. You must show the **scope** of your opinion, and how it fits with other opinions, so:
   - Conclude your essay with a look at other people's ideas to show how your opinion fits with theirs.

Parts of an essay

An essay is only as good as its introduction. An introduction must be followed by a number of pieces of evidence (the 'body of the essay'). The evidence must lead to the conclusion.

This chapter will therefore be presented under three subheadings:

- Introduction;
- Body of the essay;
- Conclusion.

Introduction

Getting the opening statement right is perhaps the most important factor in the essay-writing process. You need to say three things:

- What you are going to write about;
- The academic context from which you draw your argument;
- A brief statement of what you hope to demonstrate.

It is always tempting to hold back your conclusions at this point so you can end with a triumphant statement of what you have done. **Do not hold anything back.**

A metaphor for introductions

Pull the rabbit out of the hat right at the beginning. Show your reader the rabbit, so you can spend the rest of the essay describing your 'common burrowing rodent'.

Focus

What you are trying to do when you write the introduction is to focus in on the little bit of information about which you are going to argue an opinion. So your reader will need to:

- Know what you are going to write about;
- Know how your argument fits with what has already been written about the subject;
- Read a brief statement of what you hope to demonstrate.

Try to use the word 'demonstrate'. You are not going to **prove** *anything, you are going to demonstrate that your argument is not out of the question.*

Think about your reader

There is nothing more frustrating than trying to understand why this or that little piece of information has been mentioned in an essay without first knowing where the argument is going.

Sell yourself

You wouldn't buy, say, a car or a computer without first finding out about its specifications. You need to know what it can do *before* you shell out your hard-earned cash.

Imagine that the introduction is the advertising brochure for your essay. In it you must give all the information that will help your reader to buy your argument.

The introduction, like the brochure, is not the argument itself, but must say what the argument is going to be, and why it is a good argument. **The introduction must say why the argument is worth believing.**

What should not go into an introduction

||||||||||||||||||||||||||||||||||||

REMEMBER!

When writing your introduction remember to

■ *think about your reader*
■ *sell yourself*
■ *be selective*
■ *be clear*
■ *be concise*

There is no space for a general statement about the whole topic before you get going on the nitty-gritty.

Imagine a brochure for a sports car that started with a history of the first hundred years of the automobile. You would think to yourself: I don't need to know this. I want to know about the sports car I have my eye on.

Wording the introduction

While writing your introduction, keep in your mind the words:

■ 'This essay will argue that …'

In this way you will quickly focus in on what you have to say and avoid irrelevance.

How long should the introduction be?

Take time on the introduction. You should mention all the sources you have read that you think are relevant, and point out the ins and outs of their arguments. But you should end with a clear statement of what you are going to argue in your essay. Base the introduction on the 100-word outline arguments you saw in the 'Developing the argument' section in Chapter 3.

Remember that you can argue **for** or **against** the statement in the question. You can even argue both for **and** against the statement in the question, so long as you say why you think both are true. And it is the introduction where you should say this.

Your introduction can be as long as 500 or 600 words in a 2,000-word essay and should make up one paragraph.

Example introduction

Here is an example of an introduction for your essay 'How far did Handel's music evolve during his time in London?', based on the notes you took in the last chapter and other research:

> This essay will argue that Handel's music evolved comprehensively while he was in London, following the changes in English musical fashion and due to the politics of English music performance. It will further argue that the product of his musical evolution—the English Oratorio—was successful because it appealed to the growing sense of religiously inspired English nationalism in the mid-eighteenth century. One of the most enduring myths about Handel's *Messiah* is that George II stood up during the first performance of the 'Hallelujah' chorus. His action (which has until recently been repeated at all performances of the oratorio) commanded his estranged son, Frederick Prince of Wales, with his cronies who made up the opera party, to stand also. At a stroke Italian opera fell out of fashion and the English oratorio was born. Donald Burrows's biography of Handel does much to dispel such nonsense. Instead, he suggests that Handel was a hardheaded businessman who found success with a more economically viable musical form. The biography argues that Handel took advantage of the financial collapse of Prince Frederick's Middlesex opera company, with its expensive productions and Italian prima donnas. Instead, he put on a series of oratorio seasons, beginning in Lent 1743. These had the advantage of having no costumes, no sets, and, being sung in English, no Italian opera stars to pay. All this demonstrates a comprehensive evolution in Handel's music, but this essay must look elsewhere to find reasons whether and why Handel's musical evolution was successful in terms other than financial. The first source we shall turn to, Calvin Stapert's *Handel's Messiah: Comfort for God's People* argues that the *Messiah* in particular, and English oratorio in general, offered its audience 'exciting, entertaining stories in English about the heroes of a divinely favoured nation that was readily identified with England, and a composer with all the requisite skills to set those stories to music in a most compelling manner.' What is odd about Stapert's reading of the English oratorio, however, is that while he agrees that its appearance fitted the political context of

music performance, and appealed to the growing sense of religiously inspired English nationalism in the mid-eighteenth century, he believes that Handel's music at this time was not the product of evolution. Instead, he argues that Handel presented the English audience with an English version of a pre-existing tradition of Italian oratorio. A close examination of each of the arguments of Burrows and Stapert will demonstrate that a position somewhere between the two, which accepts Handel's musical evolution, but at the same time, which points to a growing sense of nationalism in England, gives the best answer to the question as to how far Handel's music evolved in London in the 1740s. It was comprehensive and successful. Evidence from Todd Gilman's article 'Arne, Handel, the Beautiful, and the Sublime' will be presented to make this point clear. Gilman argues that Handel was not alone in altering his style of music to capture the growing fervour of nationalism in the mid-eighteenth century. Thomas Augustine Arne wrote the indelible favourite 'Rule Britannia!' (part of an opera, *Alfred*) to suit the same political climate and at the same time that Handel turned to writing English oratorio. But Arne was writing English opera for private performance for Frederick, Prince of Wales at his home at Cliveden, and his work has largely disappeared from the repertoire. On the other hand, Handel wrote English oratorio to help a wide theatre-going audience feel good about their country, and his oratorios are still regularly performed.

(594 words)

The body of the essay

If you have written a good introduction, the main part of your essay will not be so hard. It will fill in the technical details of the argument after the 'glossy photos' of the brochure you laid out in the introduction.

What each paragraph should contain

To make sure you remain relevant throughout your essay, each paragraph of the body of your essay should:

- Present some evidence;
- Say where the evidence came from (**context**);
- Say why that evidence is part of your argument (**comment**).

What is evidence?

The evidence in each paragraph is the outcome of your research. It could be:

- In the form of a quotation from a book or academic journal;
- Data from an experiment or field trip;
- From observations of some other type: questionnaires, images, films, videos etc.

Presenting evidence

Both **context** and **comment** are necessary for your argument. There is no point in giving evidence without saying why it fits into your argument. Nor is there any point in repeating your argument without giving evidence to support it.

Thus, each paragraph of your essay will be quite similar. Each will give contextualized evidence and weave that evidence into the cloth of the argument.

Keep on adding paragraphs until enough evidence is given for the argument to be deemed worthwhile. I would say five or six pieces of evidence are enough for a 2,000-word essay.

Example paragraph

Here is an example of a paragraph from your essay 'How far did Handel's music evolve during his time in London?' based on the notes you took in the last chapter. Each paragraph of the body of an essay should read something like this, **evidence** followed by **opinion**:

> In the much-extended second edition of his biography, Donald Burrows tells us that Handel's turn to writing sacred oratorio marked a comprehensive evolution in his music, and notes the immediate success of that evolution in financial terms. He writes that
>
> > Handel's performances in 1743 and 1744, presented as Lenten 'oratorio seasons', … established a new pattern for his professional career … [which] At 24 performances, … was still only about half the number that had been conventional for opera seasons, but it represented a considerable speculative challenge in relation to the London audience.
>
> Here, Burrows draws our attention to Handel's shift to writing religious music for what he calls 'oratorio seasons'. These seasons of 24 performances, being limited to Lent

(40 days a year), were much more frequent than the 48 performances in the opera season, which lasted about 196 days a year. We can conclude from this evidence that either a few people must have been willing to buy more oratorio tickets than opera tickets, or more people bought oratorio tickets than did opera tickets. Whichever, more tickets sold in the shorter season demonstrates the evolution in Handel's music was successful. What is important here is that the oratorios were performed during Lent, a time which would appeal to the audience's religious sense of repentance and self-denial. In other words, Handel might be argued to have written music to appeal to the conscience of the British nation. Mrs Delany tells us that this appeal was successful when she tells her friend Mrs Dewes that 'the oratorios fill well'.

(259 words)

There are **FOUR** parts to the paragraph:

1. An **introduction** to the evidence stating why it is relevant to the essay topic.
2. A quotation from your research.
3. A restatement of the quotation in different words.
   - It is important **ALWAYS** to rewrite quotes so your reader can understand what the quote means in the context of your essay.
4. A statement of why the quotation fits with your **OPINION**.
   - This should take up about half of the paragraph.

See Chapter 5 for a more detailed account of this paragraph.

How many paragraphs should I write?

This example paragraph is about 206 words long (excluding the quote). Six like it will give a word count of about 1,200 words, and with the introduction and conclusion, you will have a 2,000-word essay.

How different should each paragraph be?

It is tempting, when you get to the body of your essay, to begin a new argument in each paragraph. You might think that you are giving a different angle on the problem, which will highlight the problem in an interesting way.

THIS IS NOT TRUE

This method clouds the issue, so that your reader will wonder what is being argued in the whole piece. By starting on a new argument in each paragraph, what you are doing is writing six (or more) 'essaylets' rather than presenting a coherent argument. Each piece of evidence should be used to support **one** argument.

Conclusion

The conclusion is the easiest part of an essay. It should restate that the preceding argument is valid, and why. In other words it should repeat the introduction, though it should be briefer.

The conclusion is also the hardest part of the essay. In addition to restating the argument, you need to point out where your argument stands with respect to other ideas about the same topic.

What should go in the conclusion?

The conclusion is where you can bring in any other research you carried out, but did not quote in the body of your essay since it was not relevant to your argument.

In the conclusion you can state that your essay does not agree with the argument in this or that book, and explain why.

Then you must say why you think your argument is better, or maybe equally good. Once again, you cannot deal with all the other arguments there are; choose one or two, and stop after 200 or 300 words. Again, the conclusion should make up one paragraph.

What should not go in the conclusion?

Take extra care in your conclusion that you do not say anything that you have not made an argument for in the rest of the essay.

Do not draw general conclusions from your evidence.

If, for instance, you have been writing an essay 'How important is the factor of impact in marketing communications?' you will have given evidence from, say, one or two marketing campaigns.

However, just because a particular strategy has been successfully employed in these cases does not mean that the strategy is infallible.

Imagine if all advertising slogans were almost the same: 'Eat ... it tastes sooo good.'; 'Drink ... it tastes sooo good.' The impact would soon fade away.

You can conclude with some certainty that the campaigns you chose were successful or unsuccessful because of the strategies used.

You cannot conclude that all campaigns which use the successful strategy will be successful, nor that an unsuccessful strategy will not bear fruit in other circumstances.

Draw your **conclusions** only from the **evidence** you have presented.

- You have not solved all the problems of the topic.
- Do not claim you have.

Leave other options open: such as the fact that you might be wrong.

Example conclusion

Here is an example of a conclusion for your essay 'How far did Handel's music evolve during his time in London?' based on the introduction and paragraph above:

What we have seen from the evidence of Donald Burrows, Calvin Stapert, and Todd Gilman, along with analyses of Handel's musical settings of Charles Jennens' libretti, demonstrates that it is not out of the question to argue that Handel's reaction to the particular constraints of mid-eighteenth century musical production and to the contemporary political context produced a comprehensive evolution in his output. What is more, we have seen that his evolution from writing Italian secular music to English sacred music was hugely successful since it fitted a growing mood of nationalism. What is more difficult to ascertain, however, is whether the 'growing mood' of nationalism was contemporary with Handel, or was a product of the Victorian era, the era which produced the stories about Handel's inspired writing of *Messiah* and of King George II standing up on hearing the 'Hallelujah' chorus. This is a problem with trying to draw general conclusions from the work of just one composer, no matter how influential he was or is. It is only when we compare his work with his contemporaries, such as Arne, that we see how typical was this development in English music and how it reflected the English character.

Chapter summary

Template for an essay

Introduction

(600 words)

Should contain:

- Information context of the topic;
- Your opinion;
- Critical framework.

Remember the phrase 'This essay will argue that ...'

You can write this section of the essay first,
OR
you may prefer to write the body of the essay first and write the Introduction afterwards.

Body of the essay

(Six (or so) paragraphs of 200 words)

Each should contain:

- Evidence;
- Context—where does the evidence come from?
- Comment—how does the evidence fit your opinion?

Conclusion

(200 words)

- Restatement of the argument, showing why it works and why it does not.

5 Getting the words in the right order

Words and sentences are the building blocks of the essay. Which words you choose and how they are put together into sentences can either make your argument clear or render it incomprehensible.

- The right choice of word is the key to **clarity** in an essay.
- **Brevity** is the key to writing clear sentences.

But first of all you must simply get down on paper what you want to say.

Drafting

No essay can be written perfectly at one go. You will need to write a series of drafts (at least two), to make sure you are as clear as you can be.

The first draft

When you have chosen your essay title, done your research, and sketched out your argument, choose six of the best quotes and note down what you want to argue in each paragraph as quickly as you can.

- Don't think too hard about this—just write automatically.
- Base the draft on as much of the research you've done as possible.

Think about why each of the six quotes you've chosen was important to you, and write down quickly why you think it can be used as **evidence** for your **opinion**. There is no need to try to make well-formed sentences; just get the ideas down.

- ▪ , If you don't type quickly, write it on paper.
- ▪ If you need to look something else up, use the most easily available source.

This process will form the basis for each paragraph.

Let's work from one of the quotes taken in the last chapter:

> Handel's performances in 1743 and 1744, presented as Lenten 'oratorio seasons' … established a new pattern for his professional career … [which] At 24 performances … was still only about half the number that had been conventional for opera seasons, but it represented a considerable speculative challenge in relation to the London audience.

First draft example:

Oratorios are a new pattern, so H's evolution is comprehensive. But how can I show it's successful too? What is Lent? (Wikipedia) Lent is an observance in the liturgical year of many Christian denominations, lasting for a period of approximately six weeks leading up to Easter.

What is it for? Repentance and self-denial.

How long is Lent? Forty days.

How long is the opera season? (*The London Stage*, George Winchester Stone from Google Books) Mid-September to April—c.28 weeks

Oratorios in Lent = 24 (in 40 days)

Operas in season = 48 (in 28 weeks = 196 days)

'Speculative challenge' means that Handel was trying to sell more oratorio tickets per week than opera tickets.

Mrs Delany says 'the oratorios fill well'. So oratorios were successful.

STAGES IN DRAFTING

1. FIRST DRAFT
   Get your initial ideas down on paper.

   ↓

2. SECOND DRAFT
   Rewrite the ideas in proper linked sentences.

READ THESE DRAFTS THROUGH

Decide which paragraphs you think will be the most relevant. These will be the ones that most nearly agree with each other, and with your opinion.

Do not be afraid to discard paragraphs that do not fit with the others. If you need to find other quotes on which to base new paragraphs, check through your research notes first. After writing your first drafts you might discover that a quote that you did not think relevant has become important. Only go back to the books and journal articles if you are really short of material.

The second draft

When you are satisfied that you have six quotes and six basic paragraphs that all go together to present **evidence** for your **opinion**, take a coffee break. You need to rewrite them in proper sentences, and in language that is as clear and readable as possible. So come to this stage of writing as fresh and alert as you can.

What you are trying to do is to link your ideas together into a logical argument. So you need to be able to see how a paragraph fits together. Let's look again in more detail at the example paragraph from the last chapter:

> In the much-extended second edition of his biography, Donald Burrows tells us that Handel's turn to writing sacred oratorio marked a comprehensive evolution in his music, and notes the immediate success of that evolution in financial terms. He writes that
>
>> Handel's performances in 1743 and 1744, presented as Lenten 'oratorio seasons' … established a new pattern for his professional career … [which] At 24 performances … was still only about half the number that had been conventional for opera seasons, but it represented a considerable speculative challenge in relation to the London audience.
>
> Here, Burrows draws our attention to Handel's shift to writing religious music for what he calls 'oratorio seasons'. These seasons of 24 performances, being limited to Lent (40 days a year), were much more frequent than the 48 performances in the opera season, which lasted about 196 days a year. We can conclude from this evidence that either people must have been willing to buy more oratorio tickets than opera tickets, or more people bought oratorio tickets than did opera tickets. Whichever, more tickets sold in the shorter season demonstrates the evolution in Handel's music and that the approach was successful. What is important here is that the oratorios were performed during Lent, a time which would appeal to the audience's religious sense of repentance and self-denial. In other words, Handel might be argued to have written music to appeal to the conscience of the British nation. Mrs Delany tells us that this appeal was successful when she tells her friend Mrs Dewes that 'the oratorios fill well'.

The four parts of the paragraph

1. Introducing your quote:

'In the much-extended second edition of his biography'

- The acknowledgement of the second edition demonstrates that you've done your research.
- Make sure you USE the second edition, as this chapter is significantly altered from the first edition.

'Donald Burrows tells us that Handel's turn to writing sacred oratorio marked a comprehensive evolution in his music, and notes the immediate success of that evolution in financial terms.'

- Here, the words 'comprehensive' and 'successful' show that Burrows agrees with your opinion.
- BUT you've yet to explain how 'in financial terms' fits with Burrows's wording 'speculative challenge'.
- That is what this paragraph will bring to the essay.

2. Your quote:

'Handel's performances in 1743 and 1744, presented as Lenten 'oratorio seasons' … established a new pattern for his professional career … [which] At 24 performances … was still only about half the number that had been conventional for opera seasons, but it represented a considerable speculative challenge in relation to the London audience."

- NOTE the use of ellipses (three dots …) showing where words have been missed out.
- NOTE the use of [square brackets] to draw attention to words you've put in to make grammatical sense of the quote's two sentences.

3. A restatement of the quote in your own words:

'Here, Burrows draws our attention to Handel's shift to writing religious music for what he calls 'oratorio seasons'. These seasons of 24 performances, being limited to Lent (40 days a year), were much more frequent than the 48 performances in the opera season, which lasted about 196 days a year.'

- Your restatement is in quite different words from Burrows's original, so it works for your argument.
- It gets to the bare bones of the **evidence** in Burrows's paragraph:
  - About the two seasons, Lent and opera;
  - About the numbers of performances in each season.
- 24 performances in 40 days is 'more frequent' than 48 performances in 196 days.

4. A statement of how your quotation works with your **opinion**:

'We can conclude from this evidence that either a few people must have been willing to buy more oratorio tickets than opera tickets, or more people bought oratorio tickets than did opera tickets. Whichever, more tickets sold in the shorter season demonstrates the evolution in Handel's music was successful. What is important here is that the oratorios were performed during Lent, a time which would appeal to the audience's religious sense of repentance and self-denial. In other words, Handel might be argued to have written music to appeal to the conscience of the British nation. Mrs Delany tells us that this appeal was successful when she tells her friend Mrs Dewes that 'the oratorios fill well'.

The important phrases here are at the beginning of the sentences:

- 'We can conclude from this'
- 'Whichever'
- 'What is important here'
- 'In other words'

These phrases tell your reader that these are your ideas.
What follows each phrase is your opinion about the evidence:

- 'either people must have been willing to buy more oratorio tickets than opera tickets, or more people bought oratorio tickets than did opera tickets'
- 'more tickets sold in the shorter season demonstrates the evolution in Handel's music was successful'
- 'the oratorios were performed during Lent, a time which would appeal to the audience's religious sense of repentance and self-denial'
- 'Handel ...[wrote] music to appeal to the conscience of the British nation'

Another important phrase is 'might be argued to have'.

- It introduces an idea with which you do not have to agree, and may argue against later in the essay.
- Mrs Delany's evidence about her husband (see Chapter 3) would suggest it was religious fervour that made Handel popular, but then, he was a clergyman.

- You might go on to argue that Handel actually appealed directly to (or even created) a feeling of Englishness.

SO the word 'might' leaves your options open to **nuance** your argument. Nuances such as this are extremely important: this is the meat and drink of essay writing. No argument is cut and dried, and it is the number of nuances that you can introduce that will show your reader how much you know about a subject.

When you redraft your paragraphs it is a good idea to bring in nuancing words such as:

- might
- although
- furthermore
- still
- however
- but

These introduce the different ways of seeing the same piece of evidence. It is here that you show yourself thinking, so it is here that you must be clear.

Word choices

Always try to use a simple word accurately. Bringing in long words can obfuscate your meaning (make it less clear).

If you use a **new** or **unfamiliar word** that you have learned in your lectures, reading, or in seminars, add a short account of what it means to you. Then your reader can be sure of what you are saying.

Sentence length

When you are redrafting try to keep the length of your sentences to a medium of fifteen words.

Word count

Your institution will set a word length on all your essays. It might be 2,000 (the most common) or perhaps 3,500 words.

What is included in the word count?

Regulations vary, but the word count usually excludes quotations from other sources and supplementary material such as notes and bibliographies. Regulations do not vary when it comes to overshooting or undershooting word counts.

How much can my word count vary?

For a 2,000-word essay, anything in the range of 1,900 to 2,100 words (excluding quotes, notes, and bibliography) usually counts as 2,000 words.

- If you write more, you will be marked down.
- If you write less, you will also be marked down.

Why stick to the word count?

One skill you are learning is precision. You have to be able to say everything that needs saying in the required number of words. So if you are long-winded, you will have to pare down to the barest minimum. There is no room for waffle.

If your word count is too short, you will be marked down for writing too little because it will look as though you have not done enough work.

Chapter summary

Drafting and redrafting

First draft

Get the words down on paper as fast as you can.

Begin from a paragraph if you are not sure what you want to argue.

Begin from the introduction if you are sure what you want to argue.

Second draft

Make sure all paragraphs are made up of the relevant parts:

- Introductory statement;
- Quotation of evidence;
- Explanation of evidence;
- Statement of why the evidence fits your opinion.

CHECK that your connecting words produce a logical argument:

thus, therefore, nevertheless, although, furthermore, still, but, however

CHECK that you have explained any new or unfamiliar words.

CHECK word count.

Now you have finished writing. You have:

- Chosen your title;
- Done your research;
- Found your quotes;
- Chosen the right words;
- Put them in the right order.

It is tempting to check your word count to make sure you have not over- or undershot your target, so you can hand in your essay ahead of the deadline. But however good your ideas, you need to make a good visual impression.

How your essay should look

Page layout

You are aiming to differentiate between the types of information on the page. These will be:

- The information about the essay:
  - The title;
  - Your name;
  - The name of the module being assessed.
- The essay proper:
  - Your own ideas.
- Quotes, pictures, and diagrams:
  - Other people's ideas.

THE POWER OF THE VISUAL

Make your essay a pleasure to look at and it will be a pleasure to read.

General comments on page layout

The first thing to remember about the whole essay is always to **double-space** (leave a blank line between each line you write). It is important that your work is easy to read.

So choose LS2 in the line space menu.

Margins

Leave two-inch margins on either side of your page for the same reason.

Font/size

Choose an appropriately large font:

- No smaller than 12 point.
- Choose a legible font (this is Times New Roman).
- Sans serif fonts are the easiest to read (this is Calibri).

Print on one side of the paper

This ensures your work is legible.

DOUBLE SPACING

Double-spaced work allows your marker to see your work clearly and to write comments in between lines.

At the top of the first page

- Start with the title in a larger font (say, 14 point) and in **bold type**.
- In smaller font (say, 12 point) but still in **bold type**, put your name and student identification code.
- Next line, same size font, still in **bold type**, put the number of the module and the module title.
- Leave a line (which will automatically be two lines in double spacing).
- Now write your essay in a good size font (say, 12 point), Roman type, not in *italics*, and not in **bold type**.

Your first page should look something like this:

To what extent can it be argued that Byron and Keats are second-generation Romantic poets?

Joe Bloggs Student no. 99004521
EL 2534: The Beauties of Poetry 1750–1850.

This essay will argue that despite the fact that Keats idolized Byron's poetry, and used it as a model for his own, both poets can be described, with some reservations, as second-generation Romantic poets. Byron, who antedated Keats, could be thought of as a first-generation Romantic poet. However, this essay will demonstrate that his themes and techniques clearly place him in the second generation. Reference here will be made to Byron's *Hours of Idleness* (1807), which contains a number of translations and imitations of classical authors.

Quotations

There are two main ways of marking quotations.

Short prose quotations

For prose quotes under, say, fifteen words, use quotation marks within the text.

Long prose quotations

For prose quotations of more than fifteen words, indent them in a separate block paragraph, and **do not use quotation marks**.

Examples

The different quotes should look like this:

> ... and at this point, we notice that where Defoe writes, 'and Chang'd the Generall [*sic*]', George Harris Healey notes that
>
>> The incompetent Duke of Schomberg, commanding British troops in Portugal, had just been relieved in favour of the Earl of Galway.
>
> From the informal way Defoe refers to Schomberg, as 'the Generall', we can see the close relationship between Defoe and the Earl of Oxford ...

Poetry quotations

When you quote poetry, **always** quote it in an indented block (however few the words), and in the lines in which it was written, even if you are starting from the middle of a line.

All quotes from poetry should look like this:

> ... although from the same sonnet we can see what might be thought of as Wordsworth's concern with the air quality of London:
>
>> ... domes, theatres, and temples lie
>> Open unto the fields, and to the sky;
>> All bright and glittering in the smokeless air.
>
> This is all well and good from a twentieth-century perspective. However, the argument is less easy to make in the light of statements that emanate from critics such as ...

Illustrations, etc.

Any visual material, such as graphs, diagrams, or pictures, must be given a wide margin, and separated from the written text.

Remember to number this material and to give a title for each illustration or graph, etc., even if it is obvious what it is from the surrounding text.

Foreign language quotations

Foreign language quotations should follow the same pattern as English quotations, depending upon their length. They should also be followed by a translation into English.

Notes and bibliography

It is vital to avoid a charge of plagiarism when you are writing an essay. That is to say, you must always make it clear which ideas are yours and when you are quoting someone else's work.

The page layout suggested above and the use of quotation marks will go a certain way towards achieving this. This is also why you always introduce quotations using the name of the author, and then repeat them in your own words in the body of the essay. However, in an academic essay, you must always **footnote** or **endnote** reference quotes and supply a **bibliography** of the books you have read.

- **Footnotes** go at the end of each page.
- **Endnotes** go at the end of the whole essay.

Wherever you have quoted someone else in their own words, **or even if you have paraphrased someone else's idea**, reference the source using a superscript number (a number above the line of the text, like this[3]) and write down the details of the source at the bottom of the page (**footnotes**) or at the end of the essay (**endnotes**).

Notes: a general guide

Whether you should use **footnotes** or **endnotes** and the layout of information in your notes should be given in your institution's **STYLE SHEET**. If you cannot obtain this, your note ought to contain the following information, and in this order:

FOR BOOKS

- Author's or editor's full name, **first name** first
- *Full title of book, including subtitle, in italics*
- Translator (if any) followed by the abbreviation 'trans.'
- Edition number (if it is not the first edition)
- Number of volumes (if it is a multi-volume work)
- Volume number from which the quote is taken (if it is a multi-volume work)

- Facts of publication: (city: publisher, date)
- Page numbers

FOR JOURNAL ARTICLES

- Author's full name, **first name** first
- 'Full title of the article, including subtitle, in quotation marks'
- *Full title of the journal in which the article appeared, in italics*
- Volume number of the journal
- Year of publication (in brackets)
- Page numbers

Bibliography: a general guide

When you have finished your essay, copy the list of books and journal articles cited in all your notes at the end of the essay. This will be your bibliography, and it should list each item in alphabetical order by the **surname** of the author:

FOR BOOKS

- Author or editor's full name, **surname** first
- *Full title of book, including subtitle, in italics*
- Translator (if any), followed by the abbreviation 'trans.'
- Edition number (if it is not the first edition)
- Number of volumes (if it is a multi-volume work)
- Volume number from which the quote is taken (if it is a multi-volume work)
- Facts of publication: place: publisher, date (NOT IN BRACKETS)

FOR JOURNAL ARTICLES

- Author's full name, **surname** first
- 'Full title of the article, including subtitle, in quotation marks'
- *Full title of the journal in which the article appeared, in italics*
- Volume number of the journal
- Year of publication (in brackets)
- Page numbers

EXAMPLE OF A PARAGRAPH WITH
NOTES AND BIBLIOGRAPHY

Here is the example introduction from Chapter 4, complete with **footnotes** and **bibliography**:

This essay will argue that Handel's music evolved comprehensively while he was in London, following the changes in English musical fashion and due to the politics of English music performance. It will further argue that the product of his musical evolution–the English Oratorio–was successful because it appealed to the growing sense of religiously inspired English nationalism in the mid-eighteenth century. One of the most enduring myths about Handel's *Messiah* is that George II stood up during the first performance of the 'Hallelujah' chorus. His action (which has until recently been repeated at all performances of the oratorio) commanded his estranged son, Frederick Prince of Wales, with his cronies who made up the opera party, to stand also. At a stroke Italian opera fell out of fashion and the English oratorio was born.[1] Donald Burrows's biography of Handel does much to dispel such nonsense.[2] Instead, he suggests that Handel was a hardheaded businessman who found success with a more economically viable musical form. The biography argues that Handel took advantage of the financial collapse of Prince Frederick's Middlesex opera company, with its expensive productions and Italian prima donnas. In its stead, he put on a series of oratorio seasons, beginning in Lent 1743. These had the advantage of having no costumes, no sets, and, being sung in English, no Italian opera stars to pay. All this demonstrates a comprehensive evolution in Handel's music, but this essay must look elsewhere to find reasons whether and why Handel's musical evolution was successful in terms other than financial. The first source we shall turn to, Calvin Stapert's *Handel's Messiah: Comfort for God's People*[3] argues that the *Messiah* in particular, and English oratorio in general, offered its audience 'exciting, entertaining stories in English about the heroes of a divinely favoured nation that was readily identified with England, and a composer with all the requisite skills to set those stories to music in a most compelling manner'.[4] What is odd about Stapert's reading of the English oratorio, however, is that while he agrees that its appearance fitted the political context of music performance, and appealed to the growing sense of religiously inspired English nationalism in the mid-eighteenth century, he believes that Handel's music at this time was not the product of evolution. Instead, he argues that Handel presented the English audience with an English version of a pre-existing tradition of Italian oratorio. A close examination of each of the arguments of Burrows and Stapert will demonstrate that a position somewhere between the two, which accepts Handel's musical evolution, but at the same time, which points to a growing sense of nationalism in England, gives the best answer to the question as to how far Handel's music evolved in London in the 1740s. It was comprehensive and successful. Evidence from Todd Gilman's article 'Arne, Handel, the Beautiful, and the

Sublime' will be presented to make this point clear.[5] Gilman argues that Handel was not alone in altering his style of music to capture the growing fervour of nationalism in the mid-eighteenth century. Thomas Augustine Arne wrote the indelible favourite 'Rule Britannia!' (part of an opera, *Alfred*) to suit the same political climate and at the same time that Handel turned to writing English oratorio. But Arne was writing English opera for private performance for Frederick, Prince of Wales at his home at Cliveden, and his work has largely disappeared from the repertoire. On the other hand, Handel wrote English oratorio to help a wide theatre-going audience feel good about their country, and his oratorios are still regularly performed.

NOTES

1 'Final scene', *The Great Mr. Handel*, VHS, directed by Norman Walker (1942; London: Connoisseur, 1992).
2 Donald Burrows, *Handel: The Master Musicians*, 2nd edn (Oxford: Oxford University Press, 2012).
3 Calvin Stapert, *Handel's Messiah: Comfort for God's People* (Grand Rapids, MI: Wm. B. Eerdmans, 2010).
4 Stapert, Handel's Messiah, 36.
5 Todd Gilman, 'Arne, Handel, the Beautiful, and the Sublime', *Eighteenth-Century Studies* 42 (2009): 529–55.

BIBLIOGRAPHY

Burrows, Donald. *Handel: The Master Musicians*, 2nd edn Oxford: Oxford University Press, 2012.
Gilman, Todd. 'Arne, Handel, the Beautiful, and the Sublime.' *Eighteenth-Century Studies* 42 (2009): 529 55.
The Great Mr. Handel. VHS. Directed by Norman Walker. 1942; London: Connoisseur, 1992.
Stapert, Calvin. *Handel's Messiah: Comfort for God's People*. Grand Rapids, MI: Wm. B. Eerdmans, 2010.

A WARNING ABOUT NOTES AND BIBLIOGRAPHIES

There are a number of different ways to present notes and bibliographies. The style shown here is called Chicago. You will find further details of how to cite from various different types of source in Chapter 12. You should always check your department's style sheet to see what is required, and it may be that if you are studying in more than one department that each will demand a different style.

Print and edit

Reading from the screen can lead to errors. When you have finished your essay, complete with all the notes and bibliography, print it out **and read it through again**.

Read with a coloured pen in one hand, and mark:

- Places where your argument seems weak;
- Badly worded sentences;
- Mistakes in style or page layout:
  - There should be no quotation marks around indented quotes;
  - 'Widows' (where the last word or line of a paragraph appears at the top of a page) and 'orphans' (where the first line of a paragraph appears at the bottom of a page);
  - Italicized or emboldened words that need to be in roman type;
- Spelling mistakes;
- Punctuation errors.

If your computer is able, then it is a good idea to listen to your essay with text-to-speech, as this will help you understand how your sentences work together to get your idea across to someone else. I'm a blind academic and my work got a lot better from listening to it rather than reading it. Your work can too.

Common spelling and punctuation errors

Spelling

Try not to get spellings wrong. Spell checkers will automatically underline any misspelled words in red. However, there are **three potential problems with spell checkers**:

1. You are copying from a book which does not use standard spelling.
   - Eighteenth-century English can spell 'duchess' as 'dutchess'.
   - USE the spelling you are quoting throughout your essay.
2. Spell checkers can be set to one of various forms of English.
   - US, Australian, and British English spellings can vary dramatically.

- Check which version of English your spell checker is set to.

3. **A major warning about computer spell checkers**

   They do not underline words that may be spelled correctly, but which are wrong in context.

   For example, the spell checker will not underline any of these mistakes:

   - Were, o were is the wicket which of the Vest?

   It *should* **read:**

   - Where, oh where is the wicked witch of the West?

   There is no easy solution to this problem, except for reading the essay over and over again.

   You will lose up to 10% from your mark if you make more than a couple of mistakes in spelling, so a check is well worth doing.

Grammar

Grammar is the way words are put together to make a clear sentence that makes sense.

Grammar is also made easier in the days of the word processor, since many now have a grammar checker.

Most grammar checkers underline things that are wrong in green. If you have trouble with grammar, it is a good idea to use a grammar checker.

PROBLEMS WITH COMPUTER GRAMMAR CHECKERS

Once again, you might still have problems even with both spelling and grammar checkers switched on. They might not pick up certain things that are only wrong in context. Look out for the commonest errors as you read through your essay.

Proper names

When you use the spell checker, almost all proper names:

- Names of people;
- Names of places;
- Names of products;

will be underlined in red as spelled wrong.

Do not dismiss this, even if you assume that the spell checker has just encountered a name it does not know.

Make sure you have got it right.

Use the opportunity of the red line under the name you have typed to check **you** have spelled it correctly.

The apostrophe

There is a feeling in the air that the apostrophe is on its way out. The idea is that it has become so misused that it will be abandoned in the future. Until that day comes, however, you must learn how to use it correctly.

What is the apostrophe for?

The **apostrophe** most often denotes **possession**: it means that someone owns something.

It must **not** be used:

- before the s in plural words
  'Vest's must be worn in the gym' is wrong.
- before the s in verbs
  'The river flow's to the sea' is wrong.

If you want to show that someone owns something, use an apostrophe and an s.

The boy owns the book.
Thus:
It is the boy's book.
The boy owns the books.
Thus:
They are the boy's books.

PLURALS WITH APOSTROPHES

What makes it a little harder is when there is an s at the end of the word already. In the case of plurals it is not so difficult. Put the apostrophe after the s.

The boys own the book

Thus:

It is the boys' book.

The boys own the books.

Thus:

They are the boys' books.

NAMES THAT END WITH AN *S*

In the case of names that end with an *s* things are slightly more complicated. However, if you understand the logic of what you are doing, it is just the same as the other examples.

Charles Dickens wrote *Oliver Twist*.

Thus:

It is Charles Dickens's book.

If you wrote: 'It is Charles Dicken's book', you would mean Charles Dicken wrote *Oliver Twist*, which would not be correct.

Apostrophes in contractions

You can also use an apostrophe to mark contractions (when you shorten a word by leaving out letters).

For example:

Do not may be contracted into *Don't*.

There is only **one rule about contractions** in academic essays.

DO NOT USE CONTRACTIONS.

Always write words out in full.

Its and it's

In this case, most of the rules seem to fly out of the window. The correct thing is the reverse of what you would expect.

Its means the thing owned by it.

The dog sleeps in a red basket.

Thus:

The dog sleeps in its red basket.

It's is the **contraction** for *it is*.

It is time to go home.

Thus:

It's time to go home.

Since you should never use contractions in academic essays, you should NEVER use *it's*.

A golden rule about *it's*

If you can write *it is*, and make sense, write *it is*. If not, then you should use *its*. You will always be correct.

There, their, and they're

There is a place.

Point to it. Over **there**. Do you see?

Their is a possessive adjective.

The women have come on **their** bicycles.

They're is a contraction.

It means 'They are'.

DO NOT USE THEY'RE. Always write 'they are'.

To, too, and two

The best way to remember whether to use *to*, *too*, or *two* is to remember how to use the **three-lettered ones**.

Too is *too* much of a thing.

Examples:

It is 90 degrees. It is **too** hot.

It is zero degrees. It is **too** cold.

This coffee tastes weak. It is **too** watery.

Two is a number.

Examples:

Two is company. Three is a crowd.

The castle opens later. Shall we go at **two** o'clock?

In all other cases use 'to'.

Quotation marks

There are two sorts of quotation mark: 'single' and "double". They have different uses and must not be mixed up.

SINGLE QUOTATION MARKS

Use 'single' quotation marks when you want to draw your reader's attention to a word.

They are called 'scare' quotes. Use them if you are trying to make your reader aware that the word is special to your argument.

Examples:
For the purpose of this analysis of advertising strategies, the term 'impact' will be found to be vital.

> This essay will argue that words such as 'interest', 'adamant', and 'gossip' have all changed significantly in meaning over the last two hundred years.

DOUBLE QUOTATION MARKS

Use "double" quotation marks when you are putting a prose quote within the text of your essay.

Example:
We read in the *Daily Courant* of Friday, August 2, 1713, that "The Duke and Dutchess [*sic*] of Berry came last Tuesday to the Opera ..." The duke and duchess were the centre of attention of that year's summer season in Paris.

Hyphens

Where there is more than one word in an adjective group that qualifies a noun, use a hyphen between the adjectives. These are called compound adjectives.

Example:

> Eighteenth-century furniture is characterized by detailed woodcarving.

There is a hyphen here since 'furniture' is the noun, and 'eighteenth-century' is a compound adjective.

BUT:

Carved wood is a common trait of the furniture of the eighteenth century.

There is no hyphen here, as 'century' is the noun.

WHEN YOU HAVE FINISHED CHECKING ERRORS

After you have marked any errors or things you do not like, transfer the changes to the word processor.

Now put in the **page numbers**.

Chapter summary

Presentation

Hard copy presentation

The visual impression an essay makes should suggest its high quality. It is a good idea to cover your essay with a temporary binder. These are available at most stationery shops, and can be used over and over again.

Make sure the binder you choose enables the essay to be opened and read easily.

When you have put your essay in the binder, read through it quickly to make sure:

- The pages are in the right order;
- All the pages are there.

Electronic presentation

Many universities are turning to electronic presentation of assessments. They may ask you to submit your essay:

- As an attachment to your tutor's email;
- Via your university's Intranet system.

Follow the instructions **exactly**, as they will be based on your university's computer system.

Presentation checklist

It might be an idea to photocopy this page to use for the first few essays you write. Tick off the various elements when you have done them.

- Double spacing
- Wide margins
- Font size (not less than 12 point)
- One side of the paper
- First page information
  - Title
  - Your name and identification number
  - Name of the module
  - Quotes separated from text/indented
- Footnotes, endnotes
- Bibliography
- Spelling and punctuation
- Pages fastened together

7 Managing your time

However good an essay is, you must hand it in on time, otherwise your institution will impose marking penalties. This is because if you have more time than other students to write your essay, it is as though you have been allowed to continue writing after the end of an exam.

- To meet deadlines you have to plan your work carefully.

Full-time students

Most full-time degrees are made up of four 'courses' or 'modules' per term or semester, with one essay and one exam per module.

- Essay hand-in dates usually come at the middle and the end of a teaching period.
- Exams are usually sat during an assessment period at the end of each term or semester, or at the end of the year.

It is vital you arrange to write essays well before the deadline, so you do not find yourself trying to research and write two essays in a single week.

Part-time students

If you are doing your degree part-time, you will probably do half the number of modules a term or semester. You may be entitled to do only one if you want to do your degree more slowly.

- Because you will have less time to research and write, double the number of weeks spent on each element of producing an essay: researching and writing.

Your assignment schedule

The first thing to do in planning your writing and research is to draw a schedule of your term or semester showing the dates when the essays are to be handed in. Here is a sample timetable based on four modules (A to D).

If you have semesters, your essay schedule might look something like this:

| Week 1: |
| Week 2: |
| Week 3: |
| Week 4: |
| Week 5: |
| Week 6: |
| Week 7: |
| Week 8: Essays A and B |
| Week 9: |
| Week 10: |
| Week 11: |
| Week 12: |
| Week 13: |
| Week 14: |
| Week 15: Essays C and D |

If you work in terms, your essay schedule might look something like this:

| Week 1: |
| Week 2: |
| Week 3: |
| Week 4: Essay A |
| Week 5: |
| Week 6: Essay B |
| Week 7: |
| Week 8: Essay C |
| Week 9: |
| Week 10: Essay D |

At this point your essays will either look a long way off, or like a row of hurdles to jump that are looming very large.

■ Neither view is very helpful.

Your essay deadlines are nearer than you think, but there is enough time to research and write them.

It was suggested in the earlier part of the book that you read around your subject for a few weeks before choosing which essay to do. Get into the habit of working at fixed times during the week. Arrange *four* **three-hour sessions** researching in the library. These can become slots for researching and writing your essays later on. But when you start working for essays, do not forget that you will also have to carry on doing your weekly reading for lectures and seminars.

Your weekly timetable

It is best to work out a weekly timetable in which you put enough library time to read for your courses, as well as research and write your essays. Here is a sample timetable based on four modules (A to D) taught in four sessions.

	a.m.	p.m.
Monday	Teaching A	
Tuesday		Teaching B
Wednesday	Teaching C	
Thursday		
Friday		Teaching D

Add to this your reading sessions, trying to place the reading times before the teaching sessions. You may have more teaching sessions for your modules, though the sessions will be shorter. If you are taught this way, put in more, shorter reading sessions.

Your full-time job

If you treat your course as a full-time, nine-to-five job, then you will put in the right amount of work.

Wednesday afternoons are almost universally kept for sports, so there will be little or no teaching. It is also the time for clubs to meet, so why not join a club or take up a sport? It will look good in your Higher Education Achievement Report.

Keep some time to yourself and your friends, especially the weekends, and perhaps try to keep the evenings free as well. There is no point going on working all the hours the library is open. You will stop 'listening to' what you are reading.

	a.m.	p.m.
Monday	Teaching A	Reading B
Tuesday	Reading C	Teaching B
Wednesday	Teaching C	Sports and clubs
Thursday	Reading A	Emergency session
Friday	Reading D	Teaching D

With this weekly guide you have one afternoon to catch up on things you might not have been able to fit in. It is a good idea to keep some spare work time like this for emergencies.

When you have worked out your weekly timetable with your reading times, go back to your assignment schedule and fill in the weeks in which you need to research and write your essays.

If you decide to take on some part-time work, try to do three-hour shifts and make up your schedule in the evenings. Unless you're doing a part-time degree, do not take on more than 12 hours' paid work a week.

Your researching and writing schedule

You probably need two sessions researching and two sessions writing each essay. Since you will still be reading for each week, you will need to find time for two sessions a week for researching or writing since you must continue to read for your modules.

You will have either to cut down the time you read for your modules or to add extra sessions to your workload. Since you already have one afternoon for emergencies, this might be the time for one extra session to use for researching and writing. You might therefore add another session one evening.

If you have semesters, your schedule might look something like this:

Week 1:
Week 2:
Week 3:
Week 4:
Week 5: Research A
Week 6: Write A
Week 7: Research B
Week 8: Write B
Week 9:
Week 10:
Week 11:
Week 12: Research C
Week 13: Write C
Week 14: Research D
Week 15: Write D

If you work in terms, your schedule might look something like this:

Week 1:
Week 2:
Week 3: Research A
Week 4: Write A
Week 5: Research B
Week 6: Write B
Week 7: Research C
Week 8: Write C
Week 9: Research D
Week 10: Write D

There is no hard and fast guide to researching and writing essays. You must adapt this example to how quickly you work, and to the times you are free, depending upon your commitments.

Essay extensions

There are sometimes good reasons why you might miss an essay deadline. You might have the 'flu, or there may be a family crisis.

In these circumstances you need a bit of foresight, but act **before** the deadline wherever possible.

What you need if you are going to be late with an essay is more time, usually called an 'extension'. Most institutions will offer you these if you have good reason. They represent a new agreed deadline.

Commonly, you must

- fill in a form and present an
- official document

which states why your request should be considered. Such documents might be from:

- your GP (if you are ill);
- the police (if you have, say, been involved in an accident);
- your institution's counselling service (if there is a family crisis).

It is important to get the extension **before** the deadline.
If you are ill and cannot get the form to fill in, telephone, email, or fax your institution and explain the details.

If you need to see the counselling service, make sure you get an appointment as quickly as possible.

Disabilities

If you have a learning disability, or some other notifiable condition which might affect **all** of your essay deadlines, such as dyslexia, non-verbal learning disability syndrome, bipolar disorder, or Asperger's syndrome, you may inform your institution when you begin your degree and a convenient package of extensions will be worked out that will suit you best throughout your degree.

It is up to you to tell them. If you do not want special treatment, you do not have to have it. No one will ask you and you do not have to tell.

Emergencies

If something happens the day before handing in an essay, which means you cannot put the finishing touches to it, hand in the work that you have done.

Perhaps you can:

- get someone else to hand it in for you;
- email it to your department office.

Make sure you add a note saying what has happened and asking whether you can arrange an extension at short notice, or after the fact.

More about research

8

Chapter 3 suggested ways of using your library catalogue to find books to build up your own bibliography, some basic Internet search techniques, and how to read to find quotations to use in an essay. This chapter offers a few more ways of using the Internet to find information on the topic of your essay, and some more thoughts on taking notes. It is aimed at students in their second and third years of undergraduate study, when your essays have to be especially good, as they count towards your degree classification. If you follow the methods suggested in Chapter 3, then you should comfortably achieve a 2:2. If you want a higher degree classification, then you will have to work much harder.

Free-to-access Internet resources and proprietary databases

This chapter begins with a more detailed look at Internet searching beginning with free-to-access sites and moving on to proprietary databases (sometimes called subject gateways). Throughout, the same injunctions from Chapter 3 apply:

- Never cut and paste paragraphs from the Internet directly into your essay.
  - Treat the Internet as the beginning, not the end, of your research.
- ALWAYS CHECK EVERY PIECE OF INFORMATION YOU FIND.
  - Find out where the idea came from.

This is the difference between **research** and **plagiarism**. If you do quote anything you have found on the Internet, then note it and put it in your bibliography.

Advanced searching: books

Your library's catalogue is a small version of a web browser, searching among the books in your library for the one you want. There are other library catalogues available on the web that you can search for books and journals your library does not have. For example:

↗ <http://www.bl.uk>
As of 2012, the British Library catalogue has access to 56 million items, books, maps, manuscripts, newspapers, images, and sound recordings. It is also one of the six copyright libraries in the UK, so it will have every new book and journal published in this country.

↗ <http://www.loc.gov>
The Library of Congress is the copyright library of the USA, so its catalogue will list all the books and journals published there.

↗ <http://www.worldcat.org>
Worldcat bills itself as the largest library catalogue in the world. It is not a catalogue of every book published in the world, but it has most of them.

↗ <http://www.copac.ac.uk>
Copac is a combined library catalogue of seven of the most important university libraries in the UK.

↗ <http://www.suncat.ac.uk>
Suncat is a union catalogue for all journals published in the UK.

Search these catalogues in the same ways suggested in Chapter 3, and see what books you come up with. But, you're asking yourself, do I have to travel to London or New York to read these books? It might be nice for a weekend, but you do not have to.

INTER-LIBRARY LOANS

If you find any books that seem really useful you can order them via the inter-library loan system. You will need:

■ Standard bibliographical information:
   – Author, title, publisher, place, date.

- ISBN (International Standard Book Number):
    - A 10-digit or 13-digit code unique to every book, which you
      will find in the catalogue you are searching.

Take this information to your library's information desk. You will have to:

- Fill in an application form
- Pay a small fee.

BUT you'll get the book for up to three months on loan.

UNIVERSITY LIBRARY READING RIGHTS

As a student in a British university, you have the right to read books
in other university libraries. You will be able to search a nearby university's library catalogue through its website. If the university has the book,
CHECK it is not on loan, and then go and read it.

You cannot take books out, so it would be a good idea to visit and read
more than one book. This is also a good idea for vacation research, if you
do not live near your university library.

Advanced searching: Internet search engines

It is a common misconception that all Internet search engines (Google,
AltaVista, Bing, etc.) will give you the same results from the same search terms.
In fact, they work in different ways, and some may be more up to date than
others.

- Some are web crawlers, which automatically search the World
  Wide Web. When they detect changes in websites, they change
  their information.
- Some are human-powered directories, which rely on the owners
  of websites to send details of updates to their websites (which
  can be quicker than web crawlers).
- Some work as a hybrid of the two, so it is worth making a search
  on several search engines.

A website listing and describing the features of a large number of different search engines can be found at ⬀ <http://www.thesearchenginelist.com>
(accessed 18 August 2012).

If you find a site that gives you some good information, but you don't think there's enough, then you can use a search engine that looks for similar sites, such as ⬈ <http://www.similarsitesearch.com> (accessed 18 August 2012).

Put the name of the useful website into the search box, and the site will search for other websites that offer similar information.

IT IS UP TO YOU TO EXPERIMENT

Half an hour of experimentation with these search tools led me to discover two potentially helpful websites (accessed 18 August 2012):

⬈ <http://www.vlib.org>:
The Virtual Library has a number of subject gateways (Agriculture, Arts, Business and Economics, Communication and Media, Computing and Computer Science, Education, Engineering, Humanities, Information and Libraries, International Affairs, Law, Natural Sciences and Mathematics, Social Sciences) that direct you to free-to-access information, books, journals, and datasets.

⬈ <http://www.doaj.org>
This is the Directory of Open Access Journals. In Chapter 3, I urged you not to use information from the free-to-access web, but if you're reading this chapter, then you have shown that you are interested in doing research and will be able to tell the difference between good and bad information sources. Open Access journals are usually journals that have government or other funding. Sometimes they are very specialist journals of tightly focused, obscure topics—but one of these topics might be just what you are looking for. Sometimes they are the work of idealistic academics who believe that all information on the Internet should be free to all.

A WARNING

The Internet is plagued by sharks who are trying to get you to pay for something that you can get elsewhere and better. Some sites offer you a short free trial to search their '60,000 books and journals'. Such sites may be worth using for the trial period, but not for longer. 60,000 books and journals is not a large number; and why give your credit card number to a website that provides the sort of information you are paying your university to provide?

Instead, look at the information that follows about searching **proprietary Internet sites**.

SEARCH TERMS

One of the trickiest things about Internet searching is getting your search terms right. If you try to be too precise, you come up with too few results; if you are too vague, you come up with too many irrelevant results. In Chapter 3 we saw some ways of getting around this, and now we shall go into the problem in more detail and more depth. Let's continue our research for the essay on Handel:

- ■ 'How far did Handel's music evolve during his time in London?'

We will continue to use Google because it is the most ubiquitous Internet search engine and leads us to the most heuristic places.

- ■ A search on the terms from the essay question, 'Handel London', brings up links to museums, concerts, and the Wikipedia Handel entry.

Google Instant is not much help, as it merely refines the number of concerts and museum links.

Phrase searching sometimes brings up better results.

- ■ Put double quotation marks around the search terms you want to find together on a website: "George Frideric Handel" London.
- ■ This search brings more serious links to websites whose authors know how to spell Handel's middle name.

BUT there is nothing useable for an academic essay. Other searches with Handel's full name:

- ■ plus **oratorio**
- ■ plus **opera,**

bring up some interesting sites for streaming his music, and his music scores, but still little that is useable in an academic essay.

GOOGLE SCHOLAR

One surefire way to get links to academically valid information over the free-to-access Internet is to use Google Scholar.

- From the main Google search pane, click 'More' on the black band at the top.
- Then click 'Even More' from the drop-down menu that appears.
- Click 'Scholar'.

This brings up a Google search screen with the word 'scholar' neatly printed beneath the logo. Phrase searching is not so necessary here; a search on the terms from the essay question, 'Handel London', brings up links for papers written by people with the surname 'Handel', and there are thousands of them!
HOWEVER:

- A search on the terms 'Handel oratorio' brings up links for over 12,000 papers that are relevant to the essay question!

The first thing to notice is that a lot of these are out of date.
HOWEVER:

- A column on the left-hand side gives you a 'custom date range': put in the last ten years.
  - Some of the results will be available on Google Books (see Chapter 3).
  - Some of the results will be free-to-access academic papers, which you should read.
  - Some will be available only by paying an inflated fee OR through **proprietary databases**.
    - **Do NOT pay for access yourself**.
    - **Your university should pay for access to the proprietary database**.

What you will find when you click the link is a preview of the paper to read, either:

- an abstract (a short synopsis of the paper), or

- the introduction.

Either will show you enough information to decide whether the article is going to give you useful information for your essay.

TWO WARNINGS ABOUT USING THE FREE-TO-ACCESS INTERNET

Remember, what you are surfing the Web for is the titles of books and journal articles. If you find an essay on the Internet that is roughly on the same topic as the one you are to write on, and has not been published in an academic journal, **think**: if you can find it, so can your tutor. Handing in someone else's work might seem like the easy road to glory, but it is theft.

Remember, too, that some people think it is fun to get you into trouble: the sort of people who think it's fun to send out viruses on the Internet. There is an essay, for example, on the Internet that says it is about the novel *Gulliver's Travels*, but the writer has changed all the names of the characters in the novel, and has these characters quoting from Dickens—who wrote a hundred years later. A student handing in this essay after finding it on the Internet was caught and subjected to the university's sanctions for plagiarism.

Searching proprietary databases

There are two types of electronic information that your university will have bought to help you with your research, and that will be free for you to use either in your library or at home. (See **Athens Login**). Together they make up the standard online research tools necessary for completing a bachelor's degree:

- Primary source databases
- Secondary source databases.

The terminology 'primary' and 'secondary' will be familiar to you from your first-year introduction to your subject:

Primary sources

- Books, images, artifacts, manuscripts, recordings, movies, or any other source of information that was created contemporaneously with the period under study.
- These serve as original sources of information about the topic.

Secondary sources

- Academic books, articles, websites, and other fora.
- These are sources in which critics cite, comment on, or explain primary sources.

BOTH CAN BE USED AS EVIDENCE FOR YOUR OPINION.

In my university library, the proprietary databases available are:

Quick reference	
Britannica Online	Electronic version of the *Encyclopaedia Britannica*, with links to resources on the web
Credo Reference	A huge range of online reference books in all subject areas
Dictionary of Old English	University of Toronto OE Dictionary project
Dictionary of Old English Web Corpus	Dictionary of Old English Web Corpus
Grove Music Online	An online version of the *Grove Dictionary of Music and Musicians*, allowing you to browse 3,000 entries. Includes the *New Grove Dictionary of Opera*, the *New Grove Dictionary of Jazz*, and *Encyclopedia of Popular Music*
Literary Encyclopedia	Contains 4,000 authoritative profiles of authors, works and literary and historical topics, and over 20,000 works by date, country, and genre
Oxford Art Online	The access point for Oxford art reference subscriptions and publications
Oxford Dictionary of National Biography	Contains biographies of 50,000 people from the earliest times to the 21st century, including 10,000 portrait illustrations
Oxford English Dictionary	The most authoritative and comprehensive dictionary of English in the world, and a definitive record of English language development
Oxford Music Online	The access point for Oxford music reference subscriptions and products. Includes *Encyclopedia of Popular Music*
Oxford Reference Online	Oxford Reference Online brings together language and subject reference works from one of the world's biggest and most trusted reference publishers into a single cross-searchable resource

Quick reference

Routledge Encyclopedia of Philosophy	The first multi-volume encyclopedia to be published in the discipline in over 30 years, *REP* is now regarded as the definitive resource in the field. It feature 2,000 original entries from a team of over 1,300 of the world's most respected scholars and philosophers
Who's Who	Includes Who's Who and Who Was Who (1898 onwards)

News and current affairs

17th–18th Century Burney Collection Newspapers	The newspapers, pamphlets, and books gathered by the Reverend Charles Burney (1757–1817) represent the largest and most comprehensive collection of early English news media
19th-century British Library Newspapers	Contains full runs of 48 newspapers specially selected by the British Library to best represent 19th-century Britain
BBC News	Current news, regularly updated
British Newspapers 1600–1900	Searches the 17th–18th century Burney Collection and the 19th-century British Library Collection together
Daily Echo	Local paper for Southampton and the surrounding areas. A news archive (1999–current) is available
Guardian	Includes an archive (1998–current) and a link to *The Observer on Sunday*
Hampshire Chronicle	Local paper for Winchester and the surrounding areas. A news archive (1999–current) is available
Independent	Includes an archive (1999–current)
Newsbank	A full-text database for access to UK national broadsheet, tabloid, and regional newspapers
Stage Online	Theatre and Performing Arts news
Telegraph	Includes an archive (1996–current)
Times Digital Archive	The Times Digital Archive provides a full text archive (1785–1985). Newsbank provides a full text archive (1985–current)
Times Educational Supplement	Weekly newspaper on education and teaching
Times Higher Education	Weekly reports on higher education

News and current affairs	
Worldwide News	Links to national newspapers in Europe, USA, and the rest of the world
Yahoo News	Yahoo's current news service

Electronic books	
Dawsonera	A collection of key textbooks
Early English Books Online	The full text of 100,000 early English books (1473–1699)
Eighteenth Century Collections Online	The full text of 150,000 books published in the 18th century
Humanities E-Book Project	A collection of almost 3,500 books in the Humanities
Jisc Historic Books	The full text of books published between 1473 and 1799
Oxford Scholarship Online	The full text of 2,500 Oxford books in the areas of Economics and Finance, History, Law, Literature, Philosophy, Political Science, Psychology, and Religion
Oxford Text Archive	Provides access to several thousand electronic texts in a variety of languages

Electronic journals	
Electronic Journals Service (EJS)	Searches E-journals held by the Martial Rose Library and links to full text articles
Hein Online	Law database
Ingenta Connect	Comprehensive collection of academic and professional journals online, covering the period 1977 to date. Some access to full-text articles where the library has a subscription, but often the link is to an abstract only
JSTOR	An archival database of arts, humanities, and social science journals. It provides access to full-text articles but its archival nature means that there is a gap, typically from 1 to 5 years, between the most recently published journal and the back issues available in JSTOR
JUSTIS	Information Law Reports

Electronic journals	
Periodicals Archive Online	Periodicals Archive Online is an archive of 80 digitized journals published in the arts, humanities and social sciences
Project Muse	A full-text database, offering online access to over 300 peer-reviewed journals in the arts, humanities, and social sciences. The latest issue of a journal is always available, often before it becomes so in print

Databases	
American Film Institute Catalog	The AFI Catalog, the premier, authoritative resource of American film information, covers the history of American cinema comprehensively from 1893 to 1975, with full or short records for films from 1976–2011. New records are added each year by the AFI's editorial team
ATLA Religion Database	ATLA Religion Database with ATLASerials combines the premier index to journal articles, book reviews, and collections of essays in all fields of religion with ATLA's online collection of major religion and theology journals
Anthropological Index	The anthropological index to current periodicals held in the Anthropology Library at the Centre for Anthropology, The British Museum
Bibliography of British and Irish History	The Bibliography of British and Irish History provides bibliographic data on historical writing dealing with the British Isles, and with the British Empire and Commonwealth, during all periods for which written documentation is available—from 55 BC to the present. It is the successor to the Royal Historical Society Bibliography of British and Irish History
British and Irish Archaeological Bibliography	BIAB provides bibliographic references—many with abstracts—covering all aspects of archaeology and the historic environment, and every chronological period, with a geographical focus on Britain and Ireland
British History Online	British History Online is the digital library containing some of the core printed primary and secondary sources for the medieval and modern history of the British Isles
British Humanities Index	Indexes over 320 humanities journals and weekly magazines, as well as quality newspapers published in the UK. Updates monthly

Databases	
Business Source Complete	Business Source Complete is the world's definitive scholarly business database, providing the leading collection of bibliographic and full text content. As part of the comprehensive coverage offered by this database, indexing and abstracts for the most important scholarly business journals back as far as 1886 are included. In addition, searchable cited references are provided for more than 1,300 journals
CareData Abstracts (Social Care Online)	The UK's largest database of information and research on all aspects of social care and social work. Updated daily resources include legislation, government documents, practice and guidance, systematic reviews, research briefings, reports, journal articles, and websites. Every resource listed includes an abstract. Links to full text are also included where available
Childlink	Childlink is unique in providing European, British, and Irish information. Childlink includes information on welfare, education, health, lifestyle, justice, youth affairs, employment, and benefit issues
Coaching Science Abstracts	Coaching articles, from 1996 onwards
DERA	The IOE UK Digital Education Repository Archive (DERA) is a digital archive of all documents published electronically by government and related bodies in the area of education. The aim is the permanent preservation of all electronic publications on education
Digimap	Online maps and spatial data of Great Britain
EBSCO Integrated Search	Searches several databases at the same time
Education Indexes (Proquest)	Education and related topics—journal articles, conferences, meetings, government documents, theses, dissertations, reports, audiovisual media, bibliographies, directories, books and monographs
Emerald Management Reviews	Full-text journal titles in management and related subjects
ETHOS	Electronically-available doctoral theses
FAME	Company information
Film Index International	Film Index International is a major information resource for entertainment films and personalities produced in collaboration with the British Film Institute
Film Indexes Online	Searches several film databases simultaneously

Databases	
Film International Archive Federation (FIAF)	FIAF Index to Film Periodicals Plus is a bibliographical resource offering coverage of hundreds of the world's foremost academic and popular film journals right up to the present day
Fragen	The FRAGEN project brings together books, articles, and pamphlets that were influential in the development of feminist ideas in 29 countries during the second half of the 20th century.
History of Parliament	This site contains all of the biographical, constituency, and introductory survey articles published in the History of Parliament series. Work is still underway on checking and cleaning the data that has been transferred into the website from a number of sources, and the current version of the site is still provisional
House of Commons Parliamentary Papers	HCPP now includes over 200,000 House of Commons sessional papers from 1715 to the present, with supplementary material back to 1688. HCPP delivers page images and searchable full text for each paper, along with detailed indexing
Index to Theses	A comprehensive listing of theses with abstracts accepted for higher degrees by universities in the United Kingdom and Ireland since 1716
International Bibliography of Social Sciences (IBSS)	This database includes over two million bibliographic references to journal articles and to books, reviews and selected chapters dating back to 1951. It is unique in its broad coverage of international material, and incorporates over 100 languages and countries. Over 2,800 journals are regularly indexed and some 7,000 books are included each year
International Bibliography of Theatre and Dance	International Bibliography of Theatre and Dance with Full Text contains more than 490 full-text titles, including more than 170 full-text journals, and more than 360 full-text books and monographs
International Index to Performing Arts	International Index to Performing Arts provides indexing and abstracts for a wide range of journals from 1864 to the present covering theatre, dance, film, stagecraft, musical theatre, television, performance art, storytelling, opera, pantomime, puppetry, magic, and other performing arts. It specializes in the performing arts, with over half a million citations from over 270 journals published in almost 20 countries
Internet Movie Database	'The biggest, best, most award-winning movie site on the planet'

Databases	
Lawtel	ACTS: unconsolidated, texts of acts linked to OPSI; repeals and amendments recorded; reporting of summary; no direct link to journals discussing the section; progress of bills with links to full text CASES: digest of each case with link to transcript for majority JOURNALS: digest of articles from 50 titles (extra cost for full text/1990–)
Lexis-Nexis Butterworth	ACTS: consolidated, no repealed legislation; links to Halsbury's Statutes commentary; full history of amendments; links to cases discussing the section, no direct link to related journal articles CASES: reported cases (reported from 1865, but bulk from 1936) and transcripts (from 1980) JOURNALS: full text of 50 titles (1990–); index of articles from a restricted number of titles (2000–)
Proquest Dissertations	This database is the most comprehensive available record of doctoral theses from the United Kingdom and Ireland. The collection offers the most comprehensive available listing of theses, with abstracts accepted for higher degrees by universities in the United Kingdom and Ireland, since 1716
PsycARTICLES	PsycARTICLES, from the American Psychological Association (APA), is a definitive source of full-text, peer-reviewed scholarly and scientific articles in psychology. It contains more than 153,000 articles from nearly 80 journals published by the American Psychological Association
PsycBOOKS	PsycBOOKS from the American Psychological Association (APA) includes over 38,000 chapters in PDF from over 2,500 books, published by the APA and other distinguished publishers, and includes digitized content of historical significance from the Archives of the History of American Psychology (AHAP) collection. It also contains over 1,600 classic books of landmark historical impact in psychology dating from the 1600s, and the exclusive electronic release of more than 1,500 authored entries from APA/Oxford University Press Encyclopedia of Psychology.
Psychology and Behavioral Sciences Collection	Psychology and Behavioral Sciences Collection is a comprehensive database covering information concerning topics in emotional and behavioral characteristics, psychiatry and psychology, mental processes, anthropology, and observational and experimental methods. This is the world's largest full-text psychology database offering full-text coverage for nearly 400 journals

Databases	
PsycINFO	The PsycINFO database, American Psychological Association's (APA) renowned resource for abstracts of scholarly journal articles, book chapters, books, and dissertations, is the largest resource devoted to peer-reviewed literature in behavioral science and mental health. It contains over 3 million records and summaries dating as far back as the 1600s. Journal coverage, which spans from the 1800s to the present, includes international material selected from around 2,500 periodicals in dozens of languages
PubMed	PubMed comprises more than 21 million citations for biomedical literature from MEDLINE, life science journals, and online books. Citations may include links to full-text content from PubMed Central and publisher websites
Sage Research Methods Online	SAGE Research Methods is an award-winning tool designed to help you create research projects and understand the methods behind them. SAGE Research Methods' taxonomy of over 1,400 methods terms links to authoritative content, and includes over 640 books, dictionaries, encyclopedias, and handbooks
SocIndex	SocINDEX is the world's most comprehensive and highest quality sociology research database. This database features more than 2.1 million records with subject headings from a 20,000+ term sociological thesaurus designed by subject experts and expert lexicographers. This product also contains informative abstracts for more than 1,300 'core' coverage journals dating as far back as 1895
SPORTDiscus Full Text	SPORTDiscus with Full Text is the world's most comprehensive source of full text for sports and sports medicine journals, providing full text for 550 journals indexed in SPORTDiscus. This authoritative file contains full text for many of the most used journals in the SPORTDiscus index—with no embargo. With full-text coverage dating back to 1985, SPORTDiscus with Full Text is the definitive research tool for all areas of sports and sports medicine literature
Television and Radio Index for Learning and Teaching	The Television and Radio Index for Learning and Teaching (TRILT) is the best source of UK television and radio broadcast data available on the web. Its many unique features include listings for more than 300 TV and radio channels with data from 1995 onwards. More than a million records are added to TRILT every year
Web of Knowledge	Journal database covering all subjects

Databases	
Westlaw	ACTS: consolidated; use of Historic Search; (no repealed legislation before 1991); full history of amendments; links to cases discussing the section; direct link to related journal articles CASES: reported cases (1220–, bulk from 1970s) and transcripts (1990s–); Access to English Reports (1220–1873) JOURNALS: full text of 100 titles (1990–); Index of articles from 500 journals (1986–)
WGSN	WGSN was launched in 1998 as a trend forecasting service for the fashion and design industries, providing trend forecasting and analysis to the largest and most influential businesses in the world. Today, WGSN is the world's leading fashion forecaster, with over 300 editorial and design staff in offices throughout Europe, Asia, North and South America and the Middle East
Women and Social Movements International	Women and Social Movements International is a landmark collection of primary materials. Through the writings of women activists, their personal letters and diaries, and the proceedings of conferences at which pivotal decisions were made, this collection lets you see how women's social movements shaped many of the events and attitudes that have defined modern life
Zetoc	One of the world's most comprehensive research databases, giving you access to over 28,000 journals, 45 million article citations and conference papers through the British Library's electronic table of contents

Not all of these databases will be useful for your course, and your tutors will tell you which ones they use for their own research. Nevertheless, you may find the vast number of journal articles available somewhat daunting, but remember:

- Reading a 6,000-word article takes less time that finding the relevant chapter in a book.
- These databases are available to use when you are at home.
- Citing an academic article looks great in your notes and bibliography.
- So it's worth learning how to use these databases.

SO DO NOT FALL AT THE FIRST HURDLE: **THE SIGN-ON SCREEN**

If you are working in your university library or on your university WiFi system, then just click the name of the database to follow the link.

If you are working at home when you click the link you will reach the **ATHENS Login Page**, or a page on which you'll find if you search hard, and in tiny print: ATHENS Login

DO NOT PANIC, THE BUTTON IS THERE.

- Click the button (you may have to fill in your university user name and password).
- You will go directly to the Database .

Searching proprietary databases

All these databases use slightly different methods for searching, but in essence there are two ways:

BASIC and ADVANCED

- Use basic searching at the beginning of your research.
- Use advanced searching when you are looking for something in particular:
  - A particular journal article
  - Narrowly focused research projects.

BASIC search:
Choose the same sort of terms you would use for a Google search.

Using the **Project Muse** Secondary Source database, a BASIC SEARCH for 'Handel oratorio' scored 158 hits.

- CHECK the date of publication, title, and the brief extract to see if the paper is worth downloading and reading.

ADVANCED search:
It is surprising how rarely you will use advanced search functions, considering how much effort database creators put into designing them. Once again, they are all different, so you will have to get to grips with the vagaries of each database you encounter.

The advanced technique is called Boolean searching, and it employs operators which combine two (or more) search terms in different ways:

- AND
- OR
- NOT

With AND, you make sure that both terms are in the search: Handel AND Arne.

With OR, you make sure that at least one of the terms is in the search: Handel OR Arne.

With NOT, you have one term but exclude the other in the search: Handel NOT Arne.

What is clever about Boolean searching is that you can choose in which field of the database the search term is to be found. Database fields may include:

- Full-text (entire document)
- Keyword
- Subject
- Author
- Title
- Front Matter
- Main Text
- Publisher
- Place of Publication

Example Search

I am searching for journal articles about Handel by Ruth Smith (a friend says there is an article she wrote that has just the information I am looking for, but cannot remember the article title). I search for:

- 'Handel' in the Full-text field
- 'Smith' in the Author field

This brings forth over 200 hits, some by William C. Smith and some by Ruth Smith. I can narrow the search by searching for 'Smith, Ruth' in the Author field (my friend is not sure whether the article is by Ruth or William—friends never are—but it was definitely by someone called Smith).

At this level, Boolean searching is deceptively simple, but it can be a godsend. Another example: I am searching for books by John Maxwell of York.

- If I search for the terms 'Maxwell, John' in the Author field AND 'York' in Place of Publication, I get thousands of hits for John Maxwells in New York.
- HOWEVER: If I search for 'Maxwell, John' in the Author field AND 'York' in the Place of Publication with NOT 'New York' also in Place of Publication field, then the search narrows down.

WARNING

This type of searching can lull you into a false sense of security. I have just done the search on John Maxwell of York on a proprietary database, and found three of the eight books I have so far discovered. NEVER claim you have read **everything** by a certain writer unless you have spoken to the author (and even then, they will have forgotten something they wrote years ago).

TWO (FURTHER) WARNINGS ABOUT USING THE PAID-FOR INTERNET

Remember, you are surfing the Web for books and journal articles. If you find an essay on a paid-for site that is roughly on the same topic as the one you are to write on, **think**: if you can find it, so can other students. Essays from these sites quickly get a reputation in academic institutions, and however hard you try to disguise them, they are easily recognized.

There are so many secondary sources available that you might think it a good idea to take a paragraph here and a paragraph there from a number of different academic essays and stitch them together with your own introduction and conclusion. Don't. It is always so obvious where your writing begins and the paragraph you have stolen ends that the alterations in style will be apparent to anyone reading your essay.

How to take notes

Chapter 3 suggested that you found and copied down quotes when reading a book. This is good discipline. It is annoying to have to go back to a book and try to remember the page if you failed to write down a quote accurately, or forgot to note the page number.

Nevertheless, you might find some information that is not really relevant to your essay, but that might be useful for other purposes, even for forthcoming exams. What you might do in this case would be to jot down a few words that will remind you of the idea, without writing down the whole sentence.

What you will need to do is:

- Write down the point as accurately as possible;
- Copy down any words you might be unfamiliar with;
- Make the note as short as possible, but take it in a form that is going to be useful later.

A useful tip about taking notes

Take notes on your laptop or a university computer. There are a huge number of note-taking and mind-mapping software packages. Some are freeware, and some are very expensive. Explaining each one goes beyond the remit of this book, and anyway, it is up to you to decide which one is best for you. If you search the Internet for 'note-taking software' and 'mind-mapping software' you will find lists of what is available and up to date.

When to stop taking notes

You will know when to stop taking notes for your essay when you have a feel for the shape of your argument. You will know what you are going to argue. Since there is no set thing that you have to get down to pass the essay (you are marked on your argument), stop taking notes at this point, even if there are more books on your pile or journal articles in your list. Even if you have not read through everything you thought might be relevant, stop reading.

- STOP! You will obfuscate your argument if you try to cover too much ground.
- Remember: an essay should give your opinion about a LITTLE bit of the subject.

Further ideas on finding information

Remember that you only have to write your essay about a little bit of a subject. You do not have to read from the beginning, right through a book.

- Always be selective in what you read.

It may seem a pity to waste the time you have spent on finding the book when the information might be useful as background information. However, beware that background information does not overshadow the task in hand.

When you are reading, it is a good idea from time to time to follow up on leads that might be useful for your essay. Let us look once again at part of the section about Handel which we looked at in Chapter 3:

> It seems quite likely that the coldness between Handel and the Prince of Wales was the aftermath of Handel's refusal to compose for the opera company. Mrs Delany also noted that
>
> > They say Samson is to be next Friday: for Semele has a strong party against it, viz. The fine ladies, petit maitres, and ignoramus's. All the opera people are enraged at Handel, but Lady Cobham, Lady Westmorland, and Lady Chesterfield never fail it.
>
> According to rumours that had reached Lord Shaftesbury before the beginning of the season, the opera supporters even tried to undermine Handel's nontheatre income:
>
> > The Opera people take incredible pains to hurt him. It is said (and I believe true) but why Handel is shy of owning it I cant well guess, I had it from very good hands, that last Saturday the two hundred pounds a year additional to Queen Anne's pension (for teaching the princesses) was taken away from Handel, and that he and several others are turn'd out. He has poor man very powerful enemies.
>
> The number of teachable Princesses in London had diminished during the last decade, but it is uncertain whether Handel did actually lose his post. If Handel's social position in London was not entirely secure, then his decision to open his season with *Semele* was a brave or possibly foolhardy, gesture. Quite apart from the work's pseudo-operatic manner, the secular story was a peculiar choice for a

theatre programme that began on the first Friday of Lent; as Mrs Delany said, her clerical husband did 'not think it proper for him to go … it being a profane story'. But the performances seem to have been well received.

For his cast, Handel retained Beard, Avolio and Reinhold from the previous season, welcomed back Francesina, and had two new singers in the contralto Esther Young and the alto Daniel Sullivan. Mrs Delany was not entirely flattering about the singers, after attending the fifth performance:

> I was last night to hear Samson. Francesina sings most of Mrs. Cibber's part and some of Mrs. Clive's: upon the whole it went off very well, but not better than last year. Joseph, I believe will be next Friday, but Handel is mightily out of humour about it, for Sullivan, who is to sing Joseph *is a block* with a very fine voice, and Beard *has no voice at all*. The part which Francesina is to have (of Joseph's wife) will not admit of much variety; but I hope it will be well received; the houses have not been crowded, but are pretty full every night.

'Not crowded but pretty full every night' probably sums up Handel's degree of success in his 1744 season. Mrs Delany supplies the end of the story:

> The oratorios fill very well, not withstanding the spite of the opera party: nine of the twelve are over. Joseph is to be performed (I hope) once more, then Saul, and then Messiah finishes; as they have taken very well, I fancy Handel will have a second subscription; and how do you think *I have lately been employed*? Why, I have made a drama for an oratorio out of Milton's Paradise Lost, to give Mr. Handel to compose to.

Handel did not take up Mrs Delany's libretto (though he accepted an invitation to dinner on 3 April), nor did he proceed beyond the 12 performances, which concluded on the Wednesday of Holy Week. The last performance was *Saul*, not *Messiah*. Handel was perhaps not yet ready to test out the state of his relationship with London's pressure groups (and Jennens) over that work. His programme had comprised the new works *Semele* and *Joseph* (four performances of each) and revivals of *Samson* and *Saul* (two performances of each).

Following 'trails'

There are a number of names here that you could follow up on:

- Mrs Delany
- Jennens
- Beard
- Avolio

- Reinhold
- Francesina

You might look them up in the *Dictionary of National Biography*. The first three surnames are disambiguated after the first search so it becomes obvious which one is referred to in the passage. The last three are not British, being Italian singers. So try an ADVANCED full-text search of one of the larger databases of journal articles.

This sort of research might add a small piece of information rather than a line of argument, but it looks good in your essay.

Words you do not know

There are various words in this paragraph you might not know, such as 'clerical' and 'libretto'. If you look such words up in the *Oxford English Dictionary* (NEVER USE ANY OTHER DICTIONARY for an academic essay), you might find out something interesting that could be relevant for your essay.

A useful tip about following 'trails'

Make sure you are not going up a blind alley when you follow a trail. Stop following a trail if it does not look as though you will get anywhere.

9 More about writing

When you have written a few essays and are writing essays that count towards your degree, you will need to make them extra-specially good. This chapter teaches you how to be self-critical so that you can really shine.

First, write your essay well before the deadline. Then put it aside for a few days. Return to it as the deadline approaches. Read it through to see if it still makes as much sense to you as it did when you first wrote it. Ask yourself questions about the essay. Does it communicate what you thought it did when you first wrote it? Would someone else understand it easily? Most of all, ask:

Have I answered the question?

In Chapter 2, 'Looking at questions', we saw that questions did not look for a particular answer. We saw that the **coherence** of the argument was the most important part of the essay, not the point that was argued. 'Coherence' means that all the elements of the essay are pulling in the same direction. The three elements of an essay are:

- Opinion;
- Evidence;
- Brevity.

One frequent comment made about an undergraduate essay is that it does not answer the question. To answer the question, you need to have all three of these elements in balance, and it must also refer to the title.

As you read through your essay, you should be reading about your **opinion** and why it is valid based upon the **evidence** you have found. As you look out for these factors, ask yourself two more important questions:

■ Does your **opinion** cover the same concerns as the question?

■ Does your **evidence** apply to your opinion?

If the answer to either question is no, then you have not answered the question.

Examples

■ You are writing on the essay title: 'Discuss the importance of the Tizer brand and its role in the development of the marketing mix'.

Your **opinion** is that the Tizer brand is very successful, and your **evidence**, based on market research carried out in London, Manchester, and Leeds , shows that the brand is one of the most successful soft drinks in the UK.

You have **not** answered the question. Your **evidence** is in order, but your **opinion** does not explore the role of the brand name in the 'marketing mix'.

The 'marketing mix' in the title suggests that there are a number of factors in the company strategy to sell the product. The question asks you to evaluate the Tizer brand, with relationship to the rest of the 'marketing mix'. By demonstrating that Tizer is one of the most successful drinks in the UK, you have only gone halfway to fulfilling what has been asked. We need to know how much a drink being called 'Tizer' is important in making it successful. However good your **evidence**, if your **opinion** does not have any bearing on what the question is after, you have not answered the question.

■ You are answering the question: 'To what extent can it be argued that Byron and Keats are second-generation Romantic poets?'

Your **opinion** is that Byron and Keats are second-generation Romantic poets, and your **evidence** states that Keats and Byron do not write poetry that fits with the model of first-generation Romantic poets.

You have **not** answered the question. Your **evidence** does not back up your **opinion**.

Whether Keats and Byron are or are not thought to be second-generation Romantic poets is up to you to decide, but evidence that they did not write like first-generation Romantic poets does not mean that they were second-generation Romantic poets. They may have been poets of a completely different type altogether.

Too much information

Another thing that tends to go wrong in undergraduate essays is that they bring in too much information. When you have researched and found a number of ideas, it is tempting to put all of them into your essay. This can lead to the argument being squeezed out in favour of a list of the facts you have found.

A list is not an essay, since an essay is an **opinion** based upon **evidence** about **a little bit of the subject**. Remember that **brevity** is the third element of the definition of an essay when you are reading through.

You are not trying to say everything there is to say about your subject. Put in the evidence that is relevant to making your argument—and no more. Extra information will be irrelevant, and will just waste your word allowance. An essay that is padded out in this way is easy for a marker to spot.

In effect what you are trying to do in each of the six paragraphs of your essay is to say the same thing—six times. The thing you are saying is your opinion; what will differ is the evidence you give in each paragraph to back up your opinion.

You will not waste the research you have done by leaving it out of an essay. It might be useful in an exam. It might just be interesting to know.

Drafting and redrafting

An essay is never complete. It can always be improved. You have to make it as good as it can be in the time you have available.

At this stage you might still feel that there could be improvements. This is when you can feel very alone. Writing is one of the few things people do alone—even though it is for the purpose of communication. If you feel dissatisfied with your ideas, you could always try the following strategies.

Talk about the essay before you write it

When planning your essay, you might like to discuss it to make sure that your argument is going to work. When you have chosen which evidence you are going to use, and have finished your introduction, make an appointment to see your tutor. Do not take a first draft, just the introduction and the evidence. If you have talked about your strategy for arguing beforehand, you will feel more able to respond to the comments you get when you have written the essay.

Show your finished essay to someone

When you have written a first draft of your essay and read it through, you might find that you like what you have written. It is a good idea at this stage to give it to someone else to read. Do not choose a person on your course; find someone who knows nothing about your topic, but whose judgement you can trust.

If they cannot understand it, it may be because you are trying to be too complex. Always try to be as clear and concise as you can, so that your essay is as easily comprehensible as it can be.

Some common errors to look out for

Lecturers and tutors throughout the country see errors like these regularly.

Long sentences

Some people think it is a sign of intellectual achievement to write long, compound sentences, full of difficult and obscure words, and with spiralling sub-clauses, which, it is claimed, are the only vehicles for the maintenance of the required level of academic precision, while at the same time also allowing space for comprehension in a single stroke, like that of light striking 'upon the figured leaf', and hence such sentences bring together the divergent oppositional syntagmatic structures at micro and macro levels, so necessary for the undergraduate essay.

Long sentences (like the last one) can be wholly incomprehensible to readers.

What to do with long sentences

One problem with the long sentence just given, is that you need to read it three times (at least) to understand what it is trying to say. The sentence that follows it has twelve words. It is also much clearer than the first. So write short sentences.

How to write for your reader

As far as the long sentence above is concerned, you might redraft it thus:

> Some people think long words and sentences are the best for undergraduate essays. The argument is based on two ideas. First, long words and sentences are claimed to be models of academic precision. In other words, they function in the same way as a microscope. Details that are not at first visible become clear. This might be called the long sentence functioning on a 'micro' level.
>
> Second, long sentences are also said to give a total picture. That is to say, long sentences act like a wide-angle camera lens, which might capture the view of a whole town in a single shot. This would be termed the long sentence functioning on a 'macro' level. By doing both at once, sentences constructed of long words are thought best.

What you will also have noticed is that the argument in this breakdown of the long sentence is not only easier to read; it is also clearer on the details, and gives a clearer 'total picture'. It also takes up more words, so will fill up your word count more quickly.

- ■ If you find you have long sentences in the draft of your essay, break them up into their component pieces.

Long words

Another problem with the long sentence in the example is that your reader might need to look up some of the words in a dictionary in order to understand them.

divergent oppositional syntagmatic structures at micro and macro levels

This is horrible.

A 'syntagmatic structure' is a sentence: say so.

'Divergent' sentences are sentences that say different things: say so.

'Micro and macro levels' are details and whole pictures: say so.

DO NOT HIDE WHAT YOU ARE TRYING TO SAY IN LONG WORDS OR JARGON

Use readily readable words when you can.

Another strategy for writing essays

In Chapter 4, we looked at a method of writing an essay by working out what you were going to argue, and writing an introduction which encapsulated it. It is sometimes the case that you do not know exactly what you want to argue until you have argued it. If so you will need another strategy for writing your essay.

Writing the body first

If you still feel at a loss about what you are going to argue after you have gathered your evidence, and cannot think of what your opinion might be, try writing a couple of paragraphs from the body of the essay.

In Chapter 4, we learned that each paragraph should:

- present some **evidence**;
- say where the evidence came from (**context**);
- then say why that evidence is part of the argument (**comment**).

This procedure was to make sure you remained relevant to your introduction throughout your essay.

It is also possible to **reverse the process**. If you write a paragraph which:

- presents some **evidence**;

- says where the evidence came from (**context**);
- then says why that evidence is part of an argument (**comment**), then you can use what you have written to construct the introduction.

While you are writing the paragraph, ask yourself why you think the evidence is interesting, and what you are trying to argue. The answer to this question will then be the introduction.

Example

You have been gathering information for the essay:

- Explain Harriet Martineau's role in the creation of sociology as a science.

You have been reading around the topic and discovered that most of what is being currently written about Martineau is about her role as a novelist, and her identification as a professional female writer in the nineteenth century.

You have discovered that many of her novels and short stories are labelled 'didactic', and you are particularly interested in her story *Ireland* (1832) from *Illustrations of Political Economy* (London: Charles Fox, 1832–4) (on archive.org).

You have discovered that she travelled the world and wrote about what she saw. But so far nothing has suggested how what she wrote could be associated with scientific sociology.

You find a collection of journalism by Martineau:

Harriet Martineau and the Irish Question: Condition of Post-famine Ireland, ed. Deborah A. Logan (Bethlehem, PA: Lehigh University Press, 2012).

In the front matter there is an essay on Martineau's writing about Ireland, in which you read:

> Martineau's narrative innovations include expository conversations between the Protestant and Catholic clergy, between villagers and priest, and among the landed gentry. British military and legal systems are depicted as heartless and unjust, while Irish 'lawlessness' is exposed as the logical result of chronic hopelessness—not, according to the popular stereotype, due to an inherent racial flaw. (p.xv)

The second sentence catches your interest, though it does not mention science or sociology.

FIRST DRAFT OF PARAGRAPH

Why does Martineau write novels?

> Because she travels to places and needs to write to finance her travels (professional author = writes for her living).

What does she write about?

> The people she sees on her travels. But she does not write romantic stories: they are didactic (*OED* didactic = having the character or manner of a teacher or instructor; characterized by giving instruction; having the giving of instruction as its aim or object; instructive, perceptive.)

Who is she trying to teach?

> The nineteenth-century people who believe popular stereotypes about the Irish.

What is she trying to teach them?

> That Irish lawlessness is the 'logical result' of 'chronic hopelessness' of the Irish beset by religion and the British gentry, British army, and the British legal system.

Is this scientific?

> Yes! Because instead of believing in racial stereotypes (and Martineau also writes against the contemporary racial stereotypes about black people in *Demerara*) she believes that social traits (e.g. lawlessness) are due to social conditions.

SECOND DRAFT OF PARAGRAPH

> Much of what is currently being written about Martineau centres on her career as a professional writer. However, as Deborah A. Logan warns us, we must be careful to read her didactic tales in their context. Thus, when we read her *Ireland* from *Illustrations of Political Economy*, we must take careful note of the title she gave to the collection in which the story first appeared and read her didacticism in that light. As Logan explains:
>
> > Martineau's narrative innovations [in *Ireland*] include expository conversations between the Protestant and Catholic clergy, between villagers and priest, and

among the landed gentry. British military and legal systems are depicted as heartless and unjust, while Irish 'lawlessness' is exposed as the logical result of chronic hopelessness—not, according to the popular stereotype, due to an inherent racial flaw.

If the story is to be read as an exposition of political economy, Logan points out that we must not read it as the story of a stereotypical Irish family which falls into bad ways. Rather, she points out that it is a story of how nineteenth-century Irish families fell into bad ways when beset by religious intolerance, class prejudice, and political and legal repression. The combination of these forces, Logan argues, will cause hopelessness with the inevitability of logic. By extension, we might suggest that Martineau is arguing that any family beset by the same forces will lose hope in the future and fall into bad ways. Thus we must read the didactic content of the story as an illustration of the logic of how religious intolerance, class prejudice, and political and legal repression break the support mechanisms that hold families together. With the force of logic, we might then begin to see that Martineau was scientific in the sociological insights of her didactic fiction.

ALWAYS WORK FROM YOUR EVIDENCE

What this example has tried to show you is that you can work **from** your evidence **to** the terms of the question you are researching. By drafting the paragraph, you have been able to explore the link between the two and come up with a convincing argument. You may not be quite convinced by your first attempt at a paragraph, so try to write another—and another.

The introduction may be a while in coming. You might have to write several paragraphs before it becomes clear what you want to argue, but when it does, write the introduction.

A warning about writing this way

If you choose to write this way (and it is a perfectly reasonable way to write an essay) you must go through all the paragraphs you have written **after** you have written the introduction to make sure all of them are part of the same argument.

- Do not present six 'essaylets' with an introduction to just one of them.

When you have decided what your opinion is, you might have to rewrite other paragraphs so that the evidence is all used to back up the same opinion and to reach the same conclusion.

10 Exams, presentations, and posters

Examinations are one of the few times in your life that you can legitimately show off.

This is the sort of positive thing you should be saying to yourself when you go into an exam.

In order to show off, you need to be like an international athlete: in other words, you need to be well prepared long before the event.

This chapter will spend a good deal of time demonstrating how the methods of essay-writing and research that you have learned can be applied to traditional handwritten exams. For a while now, the emphasis on this type of assessment has fallen away; however, in the current climate it would seem safe to predict that exams will regain their former level of importance. But there are other types of examination that the chapter will look at as well:

- Take-away exams
- Presentations
- Posters

All of these use the same methods of research and essay-writing, though in different formats. Everything that is suggested for preparation for traditional exams also goes for the other types of assessment.

Well before the exams

The most important things you need to know before going into an exam are:

- What form the paper will take;
- Which of the work you have done on the module the exam will cover.

You will find out this information by studying past papers.

Where to find past papers

Ask at the information desk of your institution's library, where past papers are kept.

Take copies of the **two** most recent exams.

Take care not to look at the questions on one of them.

Put it away to use as a test paper later.

What to look for on past papers

The information you need from the other exam paper is:

1. How long the paper is;
2. How many questions you have to answer;
3. What the conditions are for the examination.

The first two pieces of information will tell you **how long** you will have to write each answer. The third will tell you about the form of the exam.

The most usual length of exams are:

- **ONE answer** in three-quarters of an hour, an hour, or an hour and a half;
- **TWO answers** in two hours;
- **THREE answers** in three hours.

When you know how many questions you have to do you can work out how much revising you will need to do.

The timing of examinations will vary from institution to institution. They may be placed at the end of the semester in an assessment period. They may be held at the end of the year in a special examination term, when there is no more teaching.

Whenever they are, there never seems to be enough time to revise for them. However, it is worth bearing in mind that you can be too well prepared for an exam. If you go into the exam room able to answer all the questions on the paper, you will have a difficult decision which question to answer. You need to revise just enough to get through the exam comfortably. You want to be able to choose the questions you answer, but you do not have the time in an exam to choose between too many alternatives.

What you must do is work out what will be just enough revision.

What shall I revise?

Sometimes, essay questions for a module will cover work done in one part of the semester or term, and exams the work done in another.

It is also possible that both exams and essay questions will cover work done over the whole semester, term, or year.

Find out from your lecturer which work you have done will be covered by exam questions.

If you find that essays and exams happen to cover the same material:

In the exam, do not repeat material you wrote in an essay

When it comes to calculating your degree result, the external examiner will have access to all your work. If they see you have repeated material, your degree classification can be lowered.

Calculating how much to revise

Calculate how many topics that you have to revise from:

- The number of questions in the exam;
- The number of topics you have covered;
- The number of questions you have to answer in the exam.

Example

If there are:

- **Twelve questions** on the exam paper;
- You have covered **twelve topics**;
- You have to answer **three questions**.

You will have to revise three topics to be certain that what you revised will come up. So revise **four** and you will have a choice. **Do not bother** to revise all twelve topics. You will not have time.

Another example

If there are:

- **Five questions** on the exam paper;
- The module covers **six topics**;
- You have to answer **two questions**.

You will have to revise three topics to be certain that what you have revised will come up. So revise **four** topics to make sure you have a choice if one question on which you have revised is not interesting.

You may revise a topic on which there is no question.

Comment on ... questions

In humanities subjects, you might be given a passage from a primary source on which to comment, or two passages to **compare and contrast**. You cannot revise these questions as you cannot know which texts will be chosen. If you have attended all the lectures then they will not be difficult.

BUT REMEMBER: the answer you give should be in the form of an essay, with an introduction stating your **opinion**, paragraphs citing **evidence** from the passages you are commenting upon, and a conclusion. It should also contextualize the passages with the rest of the module.

Just before the exams

When you know how many topics you have to revise, to be sure what you have revised will come up, set yourself a **work schedule**. Base the work schedule around the **conditions of the examination** (the third piece of information you got from the past paper).

Specific conditions for the examination

Check the past paper and find out whether:

- you are allowed to take books or other materials into the exam room (open book exams);
- the questions for the exam will be made available to you before the exam (open question exams).

Open book exams

If you are allowed to take books into an exam room, you will be expected to take information from them. In exams you do not have to give footnotes.

Two problems with open book exams

1. You might think you will be allowed to write notes in your book. You cannot. If you are found with notes in your book you will be deemed to have cheated and all your exam marks will be nullified.
2. You might think you do not have to revise if you have the book in front of you. You do. You still have to know the text and where to look for quotes.

Open question exams

If you are allowed access to the questions before the examination, you will be expected to have researched the exam (or part of the exam) in the same way as you research an essay. This means:

- There must be close references to primary and secondary sources (although you will not be expected to remember quotes exactly).
- You will have to have thought up a good argument based on secondary sources.

Your revision schedule

With these thoughts in mind, write out your work schedule. Exams are intended to be stressful. This is so that your work can be judged when you are pressed for time.

Exams are usually taken over one or two weeks. For example, your exam schedule for a typical degree programme of four modules might look like this:

Exam Schedule
Exam week 1:
Exam week 2: Exams for A, B, C
Exam week 3: Exam for D

A schedule such as this makes it look as though there is no time at all, so expand your programme into a day-to-day timetable:

Assessment Week 1	Assessment Week 2	Assessment Week 3
Mon	Mon: Exam A	Mon: Exam D
Tue	Tue	Tue
Wed	Wed: Exam B	Wed
Thu	Thu	Thu
Fri	Fri: Exam C	Fri
Sat	Sat	Sat
Sun	Sun	Sun

You will probably only just have finished an essay before the exam period begins. Take the weekend off before the first assessment week. Go and do your favourite things and relax. There is no point in trying to concentrate when you are tired.

Revision technique

Start work on your revision fresh and bright. And remember two things:

- This is revision.
  - DO NOT START READING NEW THINGS NOW.
- You cannot concentrate for more than two hours at a stretch.
  - Separate your day into blocks of two hours with spaces for relaxation in between.

Revision: the three stages

What you are aiming to do for the topics you have chosen:

FIRST: Take **short notes** from the notes you took during the teaching weeks:

- in lectures, seminars, reading for seminars. This will get the ideas and arguments back into your head.

SECOND: Take shorter notes from your short notes.

- Make cards with **headings** on that will remind you of the topic and its complexities. Use these to go over the topics right up until you go into the exam room.

THIRD: Do an exam paper under exam conditions.

- Use this to prove you are in tip-top condition. Use the other exam paper you copied from the library, and sit the whole exam as though it was the real thing.

Exam nerves

Keep as relaxed as possible.

- Take long periods of rest and quietness.
- Eat well.
- Do not drink alcohol.

During your revision time, work either in the library or at home. BUT DO NOT LET YOURSELF BE DISTURBED. Refuse if anyone asks you to go for a coffee.

If you have children, lock yourself in your work room and arrange childcare for the two-hour blocks when you are working. Visits out and long walks for the children are a good idea, so their noise will not disturb you while you work. You will also do well to have long breaks playing with your children between revision sessions so you can forget your exam nerves.

The revision schedule itself

Break your day up into two two-hour revision blocks. Choose the hours when you are most awake and receptive—say:

- 9–11 a.m.
- 2–4 p.m.

You cannot concentrate more than this per day, so do not try.
My American colleagues call this CMR (Chris Mounsey's Rule) and their mantra is CMRR! (Chris Mounsey's Rule Rules - because it works).

Your exam work schedule should look something like this:

Where you have the first two-hour block to revise for an exam:

- Take **short notes** from your notes on the required number of topics.

Where you have two exams in a two-hour block:

- Write out your **heading** cards.

On the day before each exam:

- Sit a test exam.

Do not work late into the night. You will forget things you try to learn late at night. When you have finished your four hours' daily revision, go out and do other things: perhaps play some sport or see friends. If you stay home to watch TV, you might be tempted to go back to your books. Whatever you do, do something to take your mind off the exams.

- Do not party.
- Do not drink.

Exam room technique

When you are told you may begin:

- Read the exam instructions very carefully.
- Read through the whole paper quickly to get an idea of what each question entails before beginning to work on one of them.
- Answer the easiest question first, it will build up your confidence.

Writing exam answers you should follow the same rules as for writing an essay:

- Think hard how you are going to answer the question, and make notes.
- Write a long introduction stating your opinion and which material you will cover.
- Then use evidence to show why your opinion is valid.

KEEP YOUR WATCH OR A CLOCK ON THE DESK IN FRONT OF YOU. If you have **an hour** to write each answer:

- Use **15 minutes** to devise how you are going to answer, making notes.
- Write for **40 minutes**.
- In the last **5 minutes** go through your answer and check it for spelling mistakes and ungrammatical sentences.

If you have **45 minutes** to write each answer:

- Use **10 minutes** to devise how you are going to answer, making notes.
- Write for **30 minutes**.
- In the last **5 minutes** go through your answer and check it for spelling mistakes and ungrammatical sentences.

When there is more than one question in the exam

When you near the end of your allotted time for an answer, finish the answer you are doing as quickly as you can and go on to the next even if you have to rush the first.

You must complete all questions in the available time. Examiners can only mark what they see; they cannot mark good intentions.

Rough notes

Hand in ALL rough notes you have written with the exam paper; they might help your examiner understand your answer.

Illness during exams

If you feel unwell during an exam put up your hand and tell the invigilator (the proctor), who will note the fact on your paper. When the exam is over **go to your doctor** and get a **medical certificate** to notify your institution of your symptoms and the date.

If you have to leave an exam due to severe illness, **go to your doctor immediately** and get a doctor's note.

Do not panic

You might EITHER be allowed to sit the exam again, as though for the first time, OR a dip in your expected mark might be ignored when it comes to calculating your degree result.

Exam room nerves

Before going into the exam, read through your note cards to refresh your memory of the salient facts. Breathe deeply and do some stretches. Avoid talking about the exam with other students.

If you have difficulty working in a crowded room, arrangements may be made for you to sit the exam in another room. Ask about this possibility **well in advance of the exam**.

After the exam

IT IS RECOMMENDED THAT YOU DO NOT DISCUSS YOUR ANSWERS WITH ANYONE ELSE, unless you want a nervous breakdown. You will think everyone else has done much better than you, and they will think you have done much better than them—there is no point talking about it. Wait for the results.

So long as you have done your best, you can do no more.

Other types of exams

It is common to have examinations of other types. These are also designed to put you under stress and at the same time to mimic work situations. Such exams are called 'transferable skills': something your university has to teach you.

- Take-away exams demonstrate you can write a report to meet a tight deadline.
- Presentations demonstrate you are capable of clear verbal dissemination of ideas.
- Posters demonstrate you are able to answer questions on a prepared topic.

When you choose which modules to do in your degree, it is a good idea to try all of these types of exam. Then you can state on your CV or job application that you have these transferable skills.

Take-away exams

Take-away exams are exam papers that you have to download from your university intranet. You will have a fixed amount of time—which could be anything from 24 hours to one week—to research and write the exam, after which you have to upload your answers to the intranet.

The amount of work expected for these exams is determined by the amount of time you are given to hand in your answers.

GENERAL RULES

Answers should be shorter than an essay, BUT they should contain all the sections of an essay:

- Introduction
- Up to 6 paragraphs
- Conclusion

Answers should contain quotations from primary and secondary sources. Quotes should be footnoted and recorded in a bibliography.

RESEARCH

You should spend some time researching for a take-away exam, and try to bring in new material. Pressure on library books will be high, so you should turn to electronic sources for your information (see Chapter 8).

THE PROCESS

You should telescope the time you take to write an assessed essay and perform the same tasks, and in the same order, that you do when you have more time (see Chapters 2–6). It should be second nature for you to go through this procedure by this time.

You will probably have other exams to sit while you are researching and writing a take-away exam. This will increase your stress. It is meant to. Map out your time so that you revise for and take the other exam(s) while still leaving you enough time to write the take-away essays.

Presentations

Presentations usually take place during the teaching weeks. Because they stand in for an exam, it is good practice to take on at least one module assessed with a presentation to reduce the pressure on you during the assessment weeks. You will have to stand up and speak in front of your peers, but this is also good practice, as you will boost your confidence enormously when you get it right (and you will get it right). It is also invaluable experience: if you're scared doing the first one, you'll never be as scared again.

GENERAL RULES

Although you are putting together an audio-visual presentation, the format should be like an essay, so should contain all the sections of an essay:

- Introduction
- Up to 6 paragraphs
- Conclusion

Use the slides to present your introduction, quotations from primary and secondary sources, and conclusion.

Quotes should be recorded in a bibliography as the final slide.

Your **talk** should give your **opinion** about the **evidence** on the slides. **NEVER READ FROM THE SLIDES.**

- If you are using long quotes from sources, give your audience a handout with the quotes printed out, and the bibliography.
- Try not to be tied to a script, but rather work from the sort of cards you write up for an exam.
- If this is not possible, then do not try to learn your script. Keep it to hand and refer to it when you have to.

You will find endless guides about putting together a good presentation on the Internet. BUT make sure that the tutorial you are using gives you a method that is compatible with the version of the software your university has in the room you are going to perform the presentation.

RESEARCH

If you are working in a group, divide up the topic into parts and each research one or more 'paragraph'.

The introduction and conclusion should be a joint effort: it is your group's opinion.

Since there will be a number of you doing the research, you might easily have too much material. Only put in the evidence that is necessary for your argument. What you leave out—and it might be all the work that one member of a group has undertaken—can be mentioned in the individual write-up that always accompanies a presentation.

THE PROCESS

The schedule for researching and writing your presentation should be written into the module, giving you a chance to talk to your tutor about the project, and to check that your research is going in the right direction. Make use of all the help you are given. You can score very well on presentations if they are slick, carefully researched, and performed in a relaxed manner.

Rehearse the presentation endlessly, especially if you have to work in a group.

Ask your tutor to watch and comment on the presentation before you have to give it for the exam, and MAKE THE CHANGES your tutor suggests.

Posters

Posters have been common in the sciences for a long while, and are only a recent addition to the arsenal of examinations in the humanities, arts, and social sciences. In effect, you write the outline of an essay and present it in an A1 format, with diagrams, pictures, and a bibliography. On poster day, your examiners read the poster and ask you questions. If you know your topic, this is a chance to really fly—but you have to know your topic very well, as you are not tied to a script.

GENERAL RULES

Your university will give you strict guidelines for the poster. You will lose marks for deviation. For example (this is copied from a university rubric):

POSTER SIZE

Your Poster should appear on six A4 sheets. This includes title, introduction, illustrations, tables and text.

FONT SIZES

1. **Title of poster**. The title of the poster should be the name of the topic you have been assigned. It should appear in the Ariel font (bold) and should be a minimum of 60 point and a maximum of 72 point.

2. **Name of presenter**. Your name should appear immediately below the title in Ariel 26 point (italics).

3. **Address of institution**. This should appear below your name in Ariel 20 point.

4. **Subheadings**. These will be in Ariel 26 point.

5. **Text**. This will appear as Times New Roman 22 point.

6. **Diagrams, tables, or pictures**. These should all have sequentially numbered captions and be referred to at some point in the text. **Captions** should be written in Times New Roman 16 point.

Although you are putting together a poster, the format should be like an essay, so should contain all the sections of an essay:

- Introduction
- Up to 6 paragraphs
- Conclusion

Use the poster to present a brief outline of your introduction, quotations from primary and secondary sources, and conclusion.

Quotes should be recorded in a bibliography at the bottom.

Your **opinion** about the **evidence** should be clear from the introduction:

- It is what your examiners will base their questions on.

NEVER TRY TO GUESS WHICH QUESTIONS WILL COME UP

- Know your subject area and remember you know more about it than your examiner.

DO NOT REFER TO ANYTHING THAT IS NOT ON THE POSTER

- Always refer back to the poster in your answers.

You will find endless guides about putting together a good poster presentation on the Internet. BUT make sure that the tutorial you are using gives you a method that is compatible with the rules your university has laid down.

RESEARCH

It is your research (**evidence**) that needs to appear on the poster.

- Make it as attractive as possible, with clearly spaced quotes and visuals.
- Make it as easy to understand the **links** between the pieces of evidence as possible.

Your **opinion** is what will come out with the questions.

- Make sure you have given a lead in the introduction.

THE PROCESS

It is quite usual for Masters students to give a poster presentation as their first contribution to an academic conference. This will mean a five-minute explanation of the evidence before the questions. The process can be more or less formal, and be given to a few or a large number of listeners. It replaces the undergraduate process of examiners reading the poster and formulating leading questions.

Dissertations and long essays

In many institutions, two modules in the third year of a full-time degree are given over to an extended piece of work, called a dissertation or long essay. This means you have a whole year to write it.

In part-time degrees, you will probably tackle it last and over a year also.

What is a dissertation?

A dissertation is a long essay written on a single topic, which you research by yourself. A member of staff will supervise progress and be available to assist you.

Going about writing a long essay or dissertation is similar to writing an essay, but there are a number of differences.

- You choose your own title.
- A dissertation is about five times longer than an ordinary essay.
- Research should take you further afield than your institution's library.

Choosing a topic

Choosing your own topic sounds very exciting, but it can also be very daunting. You should start thinking about your topic before the long vacation of your second year of a full-time degree (the long vacation before you begin the dissertation if you are studying part-time). There are several criteria for your choice:

- Is the topic academic enough?
- Is the topic broad enough/too broad?
- Is the topic relevant to your degree course?
- Is there enough published material available on your topic?

Will the topic keep you interested for a whole year?

Keeping interested

The last question might sound facetious, but is probably the most important. You will have to work on this subject for the summer vacation, and for at least one day a week for the two semesters of the final year of your degree.

When making your choice, the first thing you should do is ask yourself:

What made me choose the degree I am doing?

Whatever aspect of the subject made you make your choice of degree is probably the best place to start.

- You might have chosen to read Geography because you liked fell-walking.
- You might have chosen to read American Studies because you liked a film of an Edith Wharton novel.
- You might have chosen to read Business Studies because your family ran a shop.

When you have an idea, make an appointment to see your dissertation supervisor and discuss the other questions.

- Is the topic academic enough?

Almost **any** topic can be academic.

It is not the **topic** itself but the **analysis** (your **opinion** based upon the **evidence** you can find) of the topic that makes it academic. However seemingly unacademic your idea may be, try it out with your supervisor.

Think up at least two alternative ideas. Your supervisor might veto one of your ideas because there are pitfalls in it that you do not know about.

■ Is the topic broad enough/too broad?

As with essays, dissertations need to say a lot about a little.

Like an essay, what you will need to do is to narrow down what you are going to say to get depth.

However, since you have more space, you will be able to give a number of sets of evidence, which will go to make up the argument of the whole dissertation.

■ Is the topic relevant to your degree course?

The point of a dissertation is to demonstrate that you have learned two things from your degree course:

■ **How** to study;
■ The full extent of **what** your subject area encompasses.

What you must try to do is choose a topic that:

■ develops from the secondary sources that you have used on your degree (the **how**);
■ explores in greater depth one aspect of a topic from your degree (the **what**).

This will make the topic relevant to your degree course.

Do not choose a topic you have studied or written about on your degree course

■ Is there enough published material available on your topic?

You will need to build up a fair-sized bibliography for your dissertation. Use the methods described throughout this book (Chapters 3 and 8) to search for books and journal articles.

Go well beyond the book holdings in your university library when searching for information for your dissertation. If you discover there is a group working on your topic at another university, or a conference on your topic, then it is a good idea to visit the group to attend a lecture or seminar, or to go to the conference.

If you discover that few people have written on your subject, you might have to alter your topic of study, or alter its emphasis. The point of a dissertation is to work within a context of current research, so it might be a good idea to fit your basic idea into the research context that you find as you work on the topic.

You might even consider buying books for this project, since you may need a few by your side.

Alerts

You will be working on your dissertation for a year, so it is important to keep up with the field you are working in and set up Internet alerts, so you get immediate access to new ideas as they are published.

You can set up alerts on Google, which sends you an email (or an RSS feed) when there is new content which fits your original search terms (⬈ <http://www.google.com/alerts>). A number of proprietary databases (for example Zetoc) also have this function. Check the databases you have become used to using to see if they send alerts.

WARNING

You might think that receiving alerts will spoil your dissertation, since you might discover that someone has written the same as you. No one will have, although their work might be similar. If you find someone has written something similar to you, it means that you are on the right track with your dissertation, and you can cite the article you have found with satisfaction.

Your title

When you get started on your dissertation, the first thing to do, as you are reading through the material you are beginning to gather, is to try to think exactly what you want to argue in your dissertation.

As you are reading through the books and articles on your topic, ask yourself:

■ What do I want to say about my topic?

Try to answer in a sentence of less than ten words.

This will be your title.

....

For example

....

You decide that you want to write on ambient music, and probably on how Brian Eno influenced its development in the 1970s and 80s.

- A search for 'ambient music' on the proprietary database Project Muse captures 487 hits, and for 'Brian Eno', 70. As you go through the descriptions of the articles in the list another name keeps appearing, 'John Cage', and a search for his name on the same database captures 870 hits.
- Reading a few of the papers, you discover that while Brian Eno popularized ambient music, John Cage might be said to have invented it, though in terms of the avant-garde rather than the popular.
- What you thought was a recent turn in music apparently has a history which would be a pity to disregard. The wide range of papers on John Cage, which are up to date, suggest that you might try to situate Brian Eno in the context of John Cage. 26 papers explore the work of both musicians.
- Linking them is the fact that both used a random basis for their music. Cage's was called 'Chance Operations' and Eno's 'Oblique Strategies'.

THINK

This is the sort of experimental and developmental research you should do before you start the proper research for your dissertation. A title suggests itself from your preliminary study:

'Chance Operations' and 'Oblique Strategies': randomness and the development of ambient music in the work of John Cage and Brian Eno

The quotes before the colon are intended to get your reader's attention. The statement which follows should be descriptive of how you initially see the project.

Your title can change as your research continues, but to begin with something that will focus what you research is useful. Reading all 1,300 papers from the three searches would be onerous work, even over a year.

*The **first part** of your dissertation will be a chapter explaining what has been said about your topic.*

Structure of the dissertation

When you have worked out the title, you must work out the structure of your dissertation.

Dissertations are usually 10,000 words. It might seem a lot, so break this up into manageable sections.

- Introduction (1,000 words)
- Literature review (2,000 words)
- Evidential chapter 1 (2,000 words)
- Evidential chapter 2 (2,000 words)
- Evidential chapter 3 (2,000 words)
- Conclusion (1,000 words)

Now, all you have to do is write four 2,000-word essays, add an introduction and conclusion, and you are there.

BUT a dissertation is not simply four essays fastened together.

- **It is a single argument**.

Progression of the argument

You should begin researching and writing your dissertation with the literature survey. This will set the ground rules for the evidential chapters.

Literature review

- This chapter should be like the introduction to an essay. It is longer, since you have more ground to cover. What you are trying to do is set out your **opinion** based within the context of other academic research. That is, explain further what you have said in the title.
- It is therefore the chapter in which you develop and crystallize your **opinion** from your research.
- It does not need to contain primary **evidence**.

You should begin with a **literature survey** to find relevant articles and books. This will take the form of a set of searches that you would undertake for a normal essay (see Chapters 3 and 8), BUT it must be more extensive.

DO NOT GO LOOKING for particular books or journals that fit your vision of what you want to say.

- Whatever you find is what you find.
- Whatever you find that catches your eye is important.
- Let your research lead you in BREADTH and DEPTH.

Literature survey: breadth

As you research John Cage's music you discover that he was anti-art, a claim also made by surrealists and modernists of the early twentieth century, and in particular Cage claims for Erik Satie, a modernist composer, that 'he despised art'. The history you discovered when you found John Cage has become more profound.

BUT do you need to go further back?

- Probably not—you only have four chapters to write, and you have already set up three evidential chapters: on Satie, Cage, and Eno.
- DO NOT TRY TO SAY EVERYTHING.

HOWEVER, your title will change to reflect your new discovery:

- **'Chance Operations' and 'Oblique Strategies': randomness and the development of ambient music in the work of Erik Satie, John Cage, and Brian Eno.**

Literature survey: depth

In your **literature survey**, you are not looking for primary evidence about your chosen subjects. RATHER, you are trying to find links between them that will make a SINGLE ARGUMENT that is the dissertation.

This will come from your research into the academic articles written about your subjects.

135

THUS:

- You discover that Satie satirized the complexity of Debussy's impressionistic music, and wrote simple piano pieces (Keith Clifton, '*Erik Satie* (review)', *Notes*, Volume 64, Number 4, June 2008, pp.741–3).

- You discover that Cage used random techniques to develop Satie's simplicity with his *Cheap Imitation*, a piano work that took as source material the rhythm of the melodic line of Erik Satie's *Socrate* (1915). In the piece, Cage used chance operations to select pitches other than the ones in the original composition (Rob Haskins, 'John Cage and Recorded Sound: A Discographical Essay,' *Notes*, Volume 67, Number 2, December 2010, pp. 382–409).

- You discover that Brian Eno created a pack of cards called Oblique Strategies, which further distanced and distorted the source material from the final composition with the imposition of a strategy chosen by chance like a card dealt from a deck (Nyssim Lefford, 'The Generative Process, Music Composition and Games', *Leonardo*, Volume 40, Number 2, April 2007, pp. 129–35).

It is this sense of development that you are looking for, as it will bind the chapters together. If you were to go too far into each of the composers you have chosen, you would have no sense of development, so begin by looking for links between them.

This is, of course a **two-way process**:

- you find the composers that are linked, and choose to work with them;
- you research the links between them, and ignore everything else about your composers that is not relevant.

Then you will end up with a SINGLE ARGUMENT, as your literature survey transforms itself into a literature review by a process of discarding things that are not relevant to your dissertation.

In the present example, the **literature survey** of 1,300 articles has been focused as it has become the argument of your **literature review** (your first chapter).

A NOTE OF WARNING

The example I have given has only three references. This is not nearly enough research for a literature review chapter. However, you can also do too much research, which will obfuscate your argument with detail. Maintain a balance between detail and succinctness.

Evidential chapters 1, 2, and 3

These chapters should be like the body of the essay.

■ They give the primary **evidence** for the validity of your **opinion**.

■ They differ from the body of a single essay, since they need to demonstrate the **progression** of the **argument** which you have laid out in the literature review.

*The **next three parts** of your dissertation will give evidence from different perspectives, following the methodology you have set up in the first chapter.*

FOR EXAMPLE

After the literature review chapter:

■ The Satie chapter needs to make direct comparisons between Debussy's music and Satie's, demonstrating how much less complicated Satie's music became.

■ The Cage chapter needs to give examples of the chance operations Cage used to make the same sort of simplifications that Satie made to Debussy's music. You can then refer this to Cage's own music—for example, his famous 4′33″ (four minutes and 33 seconds of silence).

■ Finally, when you write about Eno, you can situate his ambient music within both classical and avant-garde traditions and demonstrate how he built on the simplifications and random interventions of Satie and Cage to create a distinctive brand.

Each new chapter needs its own stance that marks a progression from the last, so that the whole dissertation:

■ takes on a shape;
■ has a direction;
■ has a coherent argument throughout.

Each chapter, whether it be the literature review or the evidential chapters, ought to follow the structure of an essay as laid out in Chapters 2–6.

Introduction and conclusion

These should be written last.

The **introduction** should lay out the whole argument, and briefly state where the argument is going in the individual chapters. This will amount to 200 words on the whole project and 200 words on each of the chapters.

The **conclusion** should point out the weak points in the argument, but give an idea, say, why this argument is better than the alternatives.

Page layout and presentation

Your institution will have stringent requirements about page layout and presentation of dissertations. Follow them to the letter.

References: Notes and Bibliography

All ideas taken from another source, regardless of whether directly quoted or paraphrased, need to be referenced in the text of your essay or dissertation.

Your home institution or department will produce a style sheet, or publish which form of notes and bibliography they require. Follow it to the letter and ignore this chapter.

But if you are at a loss, then this chapter will at least demonstrate that you know what you are doing.

ABOVE ALL IN CITATIONS AND BIBLIOGRAPHIES: BE CONSISTENT

There are two common systems of putting citations in your essay which this chapter will demonstrate. They are called:

- Notes and bibliography (Chicago);
- Author–date (Harvard).

Do not mix up the two systems.

Footnotes or endnotes and bibliography — Chicago style

The *Chicago Manual of Style* is now in its sixteenth edition. It is 1,200 pages long and will tell you everything you will ever need to know about laying out an essay or book.

This is a brief guide to the basics of noting the Chicago way. Your library will have a copy of the manual if you need more information.

Whenever you quote something:

- Put a superscript number next to it.
- Write down the source:

- either at the bottom of the page (footnotes);
- or at the end of the essay (endnotes).
■ Copy the source in the bibliography.

Chicago Style for Footnotes or Endnotes and Bibliography

Each example gives you:

1. The way the first citation should appear, followed by
2. a shortened version for subsequent citations.

NEVER USE **ibid**. or **op.cit**. for repeated citations as they always confuse readers.

The way the citation should appear in the bibliography:

Books

BOOK ONE AUTHOR

1. Chris Mounsey, *Being the Body of Christ: Towards a Twenty-first century Homosexual Theology for the Anglican Church* (Sheffield: Equinox, 2012), 25.
2. Mounsey, *Being the Body*, 3.

Mounsey, Chris. *Being the Body of Christ: Towards a Twenty-first Century Homosexual Theology for the Anglican Church*. Sheffield: Equinox, 2012.

BOOK, TWO OR MORE AUTHORS

1. Purnima Khare and Abhaba Swarup, *Engineering Physics: Fundamentals and Modern Applications* (Sudbury, MA: Jones and Bartlett, 2007), 52.
2. Khare and Swarup, *Engineering Physics*, 59–61.

Khare, Purnima, and Abhaba Swarup. *Engineering Physics: Fundamentals and Modern Applications*. Sudbury, MA: Jones and Bartlett, 2007.

EDITOR, TRANSLATOR, OR COMPILER INSTEAD OF AUTHOR

1. Scott Lewis, ed., *The Letters of Elizabeth Barrett Browning To Her Sister Arabella*, 2 vols. (Winfield, KS: Wedgestone Press, 2002), vol.1, 91–92.
2. Lewis, *Letters of Elizabeth Barrett Browning*, vol. 2, 24.

Lewis, Scott, ed. *Letters of Elizabeth Barrett Browning*. 2 vols. Winfield KS: Wedgestone Press, 2002.

EDITOR, TRANSLATOR, OR COMPILER IN ADDITION TO AUTHOR

1. Gaston Leroux, *The Phantom of the Opera*, trans. David Coward (Oxford: Oxford University Press, 2012), 108–12.
2. Leroux, *Phantom*, 11.

Leroux, Gaston. *The Phantom of the Opera*. Translated by David Coward. Oxford: Oxford University Press, 2012.

CHAPTER OR OTHER PART OF A BOOK

1. Caroline Gonda, '"An Extraordinary Subject for Dissection": The Strange Cases of James Allen and Lavinia Edwards,' in *Histories of Sexualities: In Search of the Normal*, ed. Chris Mounsey, (Lewisburg: Bucknell University Press, 2013), 256.
2. Gonda, 'An Extraordinary Subject,' 231–32.

Gonda, Caroline. '"An Extraordinary Subject for Dissection": The Strange Cases of James Allen and Lavinia Edwards.' In *Histories of Sexualities: In Search of the Normal*, edited by Chris Mounsey, 230–57. Lewisburg: Bucknell University Press, 2013.

PREFACE, FOREWORD, INTRODUCTION, OR SIMILAR PART OF A BOOK

1. J. Paul Hunter, preface to *Frankenstein; or, The Modern Prometheus*, by Mary Wollstonecraft Shelley (New York: W. W. Norton & Co., 1996), 5–7.
2. Hunter, preface, 6.

Hunter, J. Paul. Preface to *Frankenstein; or, The Modern Prometheus*, by Mary Wollstonecraft Shelley, 5–7. New York: W. W. Norton & Co., 1996.

BOOK PUBLISHED ELECTRONICALLY

Cite the version of the book that you consulted, should there be different formats available. If you consulted a book online, list a URL and include an access date. You can include a section title or a chapter or the like if no fixed page numbers are available (page numbers are sometimes, but not always, available in Kindle editions).

1. Alan Hollinghurst, *The Swimming-Pool Library* (London: Vintage, 2004), Kindle edition.

2. Hollinghurst, *The Swimming-Pool Library*.

Hollinghurst, Alan. *The Swimming-Pool Library*. London: Vintage, 2004. Kindle edition.

1. Daniel Defoe, *The life and strange surprizing adventures of Robinson Crusoe, of York, mariner: Who lived eight and twenty years, all alone in an un-inhabited island on the coast of America, near the mouth of the great river of Oroonoque; having been cast on shore by shipwreck, wherein all the men perished but himself. With an account how he was at last as strangely deliver'd by pyrates. Written by himself.* (London: W. Taylor, 1719), 245, accessed 29 August 2012, http://find.galegroup.com/ecco/infomark.do?&source=gale&prodId=ECCO&userGroupName=ucwinch&tabID=T001&docId=CB3327675440&type=multipage&contentSet=ECCOArticles&version=1.0&docLevel=FASCIMILE.

2. Defoe, *Robinson Crusoe*, 125.
   Defoe, Daniel. *The life and strange surprizing adventures of Robinson Crusoe, of York, mariner: Who lived eight and twenty years, all alone in an un-inhabited island on the coast of America, near the mouth of the great river of Oroonoque; having been cast on shore by shipwreck, wherein all the men perished but himself. With an account how he was at last as strangely deliver'd by pyrates. Written by himself.* London, MDCCXIX. [1719]. Eighteenth Century Collections Online. Gale. University of Winchester. 29 Aug. 2012. http://find.galegroup.com/ecco/infomark.do?&source=gale&prodId=ECCO&userGroupName=ucwinch&tabID=T001&docId=CB3327675440&type=multipage&contentSet=ECCOArticles&version=1.0&docLevel=FASCIMILE.

Journal article

ARTICLE IN A PRINT JOURNAL

If you have consulted specific pages list them in a note. List the page range for the whole article in the bibliography.

1. Elizabeth Roche, 'Seven Handel Oratorios,' *Early Music* 38 (2010): 315.
2. Roche, 'Handel Oratorios,' 314.

Roche, Elizabeth. 'Seven Handel Oratorios,' *Early Music* 38 (2010): 313–16.

ARTICLE IN AN ONLINE JOURNAL

Online journals may list a DOI (Digital Object Identifier); this is a permanent ID that, when appended to http://dx.doi.org/ in the address bar of an Internet browser, will lead to the source. List a URL if no DOI is available. Include an access date only if one is required by your publisher or discipline.

1. Miloš Kankaraš and Guy Moors, 'Cross-National and Cross-Ethnic Differences in Attitudes: A Case of Luxembourg', *Cross-Cultural Research*, 46 (2012): 234, accessed 30 August, 2012, doi:10.1177/1069397112440945.
2. Kankaraš and Moors, 'Cross-National and Cross-Ethnic Difference,' 248.

Kankaraš, Miloš and Guy Moors. 'Cross-National and Cross-Ethnic Differences in Attitudes: A Case of Luxembourg.' *Cross-Cultural Research*, 46 (2012): 224–54. Accessed 30 August, 2012. doi:10.1177/1069397112440945.

ARTICLE IN A NEWSPAPER OR POPULAR MAGAZINE

You may cite newspaper and magazine articles in running text ("As Owen Gibson noted in a *Guardian* article on August 31, 2012, ...") instead of in a note, and they are often omitted from bibliographies. The examples below show the more formal versions of the citations. Include a URL and an access date if the article was referred to online. If no author is identified, begin the citation with the article title.

1. Owen Gibson, 'Paralympics 2012: gold for GB in velodrome and pool on first day' *Guardian*, 31 August 2012, 1.
2. Gibson, 'Paralympics 2012,' 1.

Gibson, Owen. 'Paralympics 2012: gold for GB in velodrome and pool on first day.' *Guardian*, 31 August 2012.

1. 'The Olympic Games which have been neglected for such a length of time, seem to be again revived,' *The Times*, 6 September 1790, accessed 31 August 2012 http://infotrac. galegroup.com/itw/infomark/665/802/184711040w16/ purl=rc1_TTDA_0_CS51514150&dyn=3!xrn_1_0_ CS51514150&hst_1?sw_aep=ucwinch.
2. 'The Olympic Games.'

'The Olympic Games which have been neglected for such a length of time, seem to be again revived.' *The Times*, 6 September 1790. Accessed 31 August 2012. http://infotrac.galegroup.com/itw/infomark/665/802/184711040w16/ purl=rc1_TTDA_0_CS51514150&dyn=3!xrn_1_0_CS51514150&hst_1? sw_aep=ucwinch.

Website

A citation of website content can generally be limited to a mention in the text or in a note ("As of August 29, 2012, Starbucks listed dairy and gluten free snacks on its website …"). The examples below can be followed should a more formal style be required. Because website content can be subject to change, be sure to include a date of access or, if possible, a date that the site was last modified.

1. 'Chocolate Hazelnut Loaf,' Starbucks, accessed 29 August 2012, http://starbucks.co.uk/menu/food-list/ muffins-pastries-and-doughnuts/caramelised-hazelnut-and- belgian-chocolate-chunk-muffin.
2. 'Chocolate Hazelnut Loaf.' Starbucks. 'Chocolate Hazelnut Loaf.' Accessed 29 August 2012. http://starbucks.co.uk/menu/ food-list/muffins-pastries-and-doughnuts/caramelised-hazelnut -and-belgian-chocolate-chunk-muffin.

Film

A citation to a film might be to the whole, or to a named scene, which can precede the citation in quotation marks.

1. 'Conversation between ANAKIN and OBI-WAN', *Star Wars II: Attack of the Clones*, DVD, directed by George Lucas, (2002; Beverly Hills, CA: Twentieth Century Fox, 2002).
2. 'Conversation between ANAKIN and OBI-WAN,' *Star Wars II.*

Star Wars II: Attack of the Clones. Directed by George Lucas, 2002; Beverly Hills, CA: Twentieth Century Fox, 2002. DVD.

Example of Chicago-style noting

In this example—the introduction to the essay on Handel used in Chapters 4–6—note that it is not just the direct quotations which are noted, but the paraphrased references as well.

> This essay will argue that Handel's music evolved comprehensively while he was in London, following the changes in English musical fashion and due to the politics of English music performance. It will further argue that the product of his musical evolution–the English Oratorio–was successful because it appealed to the growing sense of religiously inspired English nationalism in the mid-eighteenth century. One of the most enduring myths about Handel's *Messiah* is that George II stood up during the first performance of the 'Hallelujah' chorus. His action (which has until recently been repeated at all performances of the oratorio) commanded his estranged son, Frederick Prince of Wales, with his cronies, who made up the opera party to stand also. At a stroke Italian opera fell out of fashion and the English oratorio was born.[1] Donald Burrows's biography of Handel does much to dispel such nonsense.[2] Instead, he suggests that Handel was a hardheaded businessman who found success with a more economically viable musical form. The biography argues that Handel took advantage of the financial collapse of Prince Frederick's Middlesex opera company, with its expensive productions and Italian prima donnas. In its stead, he put on a series of oratorio seasons, beginning in Lent 1743. These had the advantage of having no costumes, no sets, and being sung in English, no Italian opera stars to pay. All this demonstrates a comprehensive evolution in Handel's music, but this essay must look elsewhere to find reasons whether and why Handel's musical evolution was successful in terms other than financial. The first source we shall turn to, Calvin

Stapert's Handel's Messiah: Comfort for God's People[3] argues that the Messiah in particular, and English oratorio in general, offered its audience 'exciting, entertaining stories in English about the heroes of a divinely favoured nation that was readily identified with England, and a composer with all the requisite skills to set those stories to music in a most compelling manner.'[4] What is odd about Stapert's reading of the English oratorio, however, is that while he agrees that its appearance fitted the political context of music performance, and appealed to the growing sense of religiously inspired English nationalism in the mid-eighteenth century, he believes that Handel's music at this time was not the product of evolution. Instead, he argues that Handel presented the English audience with an English version of a pre-existing tradition of Italian oratorio. A close examination of each of the arguments of Burrows and Stapert will demonstrate that a position somewhere between the two, which accepts Handel's musical evolution, but at the same time, which points to a growing sense of nationalism in England, gives the best answer to the question as to how far Handel's music evolved in London in the 1740s. It was comprehensive and successful. Evidence from Todd Gilman's article 'Arne, Handel, the Beautiful, and the Sublime' will be presented to make this point clear.[5] Gilman argues that Handel was not alone in altering his style of music to capture the growing fervour of nationalism in the mid-eighteenth century. Thomas Augustine Arne wrote the indelible favourite 'Rule Britannia!' (part of an opera, Alfred) to suit the same political climate and at the same time that Handel turned to writing English oratorio. But Arne was writing English opera for private performance for Frederick, Prince of Wales, at his home at Cliveden, and his work has largely disappeared from the repertoire. On the other hand, Handel wrote English oratorio to help a wide theatre-going audience feel good about their country, and his oratorios are still regularly performed.

Notes

1. 'Final scene', The Great Mr Handel, VHS, directed by Norman Walker, (1942; London: Connoisseur, 1992).
2. Donald Burrows, Handel: The Master Musicians, 2nd edn. (Oxford: Oxford University Press, 2012).
3. Calvin Stapert, Handel's Messiah: Comfort for God's People, (Grand Rapids MI: Wm. B. Eerdmans, 2010).
4. Stapert, Handel's Messiah, 36.
5. Todd Gilman, 'Arne, Handel, the Beautiful, and the Sublime,' in Eighteenth-Century Studies, 42 (2009): 529–555.

Bibliography

With the Chicago system of noting, you must supply a full bibliography as well as the list of notes.

If you have used endnotes at the end of your essay, put the bibliography after the endnotes.

The bibliography is nearly a repetition of the information in the notes, but in alphabetical order, so it can more easily be searched.

EXAMPLE CHICAGO STYLE BIBLIOGRAPHY

Burrows, Donald. *Handel: The Master Musicians*, 2nd edn. Oxford: Oxford University Press, 2012.

Gilman, Todd. 'Arne, Handel, the Beautiful, and the Sublime.' *Eighteenth-Century Studies* 42 (2009): 529–555.

The Great Mr Handel. VHS. Directed by Norman Walker. 1942; London: Connoisseur, 1992.

Stapert, Calvin. *Handel's Messiah: Comfort for God's People*. MI: Wm. B. Eerdmans, 2010.

Author–date citations

The author–date method of citation uses abbreviations within the text rather than footnotes. The abbreviations may then be checked against a list of works cited.

To link the information you use in your text to its source (book, article, etc.) include:

- the author's name in your text AND, IN BRACKETS
- the year of publication
- the page number(s) if there is a direct quotation

at the appropriate point in your text.

If the author's name does not naturally occur in your writing, put the author's surname, the date, and the page numbers (if appropriate) in brackets.

Examples

You are referring to my book *Being the Body of Christ*, so use my surname, Mounsey, the date, and the page number to cite in the text in one of the following ways:

> Mounsey (2012) has suggested that this interpretation of Wilde's religious intention is inaccurate.
> It has been suggested (Mounsey, 2012) that this interpretation of Wilde's religious intention is inaccurate.
> The suggestion that 'Wilde was a nominal Anglican all his life' (Mounsey 2012, p.11) would suggest that other interpretations of his religious intention …

Where there are two or more authors, cite only the first followed by 'et al.' (which means 'and others'):

> It has been argued (Khare et al., 2007) that engineering physics is the discipline devoted to creating and optimizing engineering solutions.

Note: up to three author names can be given in your reference list of works cited.

If an author has published more documents in the same year, distinguish between them by adding lower-case letters:

> In recent studies by Gonda (2010a, 2010b, 2010c)…

If you want to cite one author citing another, where Mounsey discusses the work of Alderson you could use:

> Alderson (2000), as cited by Mounsey (2012), suggests that …

OR

> Alderson's 2000 study (cited in Mounsey 2012, p.164) shows that…

If you find the information in several sources, then list them all:

> Several writers (Mounsey 2012; Gonda 2007; Alderson 2000) argue that …

Citation list

At the end of your essay, you put the list of works cited in alphabetical order by the name of the author.

BOOK ONE AUTHOR

Mounsey, C. F. (2012) *Being the Body of Christ: Towards a Twenty-first Century Homosexual Theology for the Anglican Church.* Sheffield: Equinox.

BOOK TWO OR MORE AUTHORS

Khare, Purnima, and Swarup, A. (2007) *Engineering Physics: Fundamentals and Modern Applications.* Sudbury MA: Jones and Bartlett.

EDITOR, TRANSLATOR, OR COMPILER INSTEAD OF AUTHOR

Lewis, S., ed. 2002 *Letters of Elizabeth Barrett Browning.* 2 vols. Winfield, KS: Wedgestone Press.

EDITOR, TRANSLATOR, OR COMPILER IN ADDITION TO AUTHOR

García Márquez, G. (1989) *Love in the Time of Cholera.* Translated from Spanish by E. Grossman. Harmondsworth: Penguin, 1989.

CHAPTER OR OTHER PART OF A BOOK

Gonda, C. (2013) '"An Extraordinary Subject for Dissection": The Strange Cases of James Allen and Lavinia Edwards.' In: Mounsey, C. (ed.) *Histories of Sexualities: In Search of the Normal,* edited by C. Mounsey, 230–57. Lewisburg: Bucknell University Press.

PREFACE, FOREWORD, INTRODUCTION, OR SIMILAR PART OF A BOOK

Hunter, J. P. (1996) *Preface to Frankenstein; or, The Modern Prometheus,* by Mary Wollstonecraft Shelley, New York: W. W. Norton & Co., pp.5–7.

BOOK PUBLISHED ELECTRONICALLY

Hollinghurst, Alan. (2004) *The Swimming-Pool Library.* London: Vintage. Kindle Edition.

Defoe, Daniel. (1719) *The life and strange surprizing adventures of Robinson Crusoe, of York, mariner: Who lived eight and twenty years, all alone in an un-inhabited island on the coast of America, near the mouth of the great river of Oroonoque; having been cast on shore by shipwreck, wherein all the men perished but himself. With an account how he was at last as strangely deliver'd by pyrates. Written by himself.* London, MDCCXIX. Eighteenth Century Collections Online. Gale. University of Winchester. 29 Aug. 2012. http://find.galegroup.com/ecco/infomark.do?&source=gale& prodId=ECCO&userGroupName=ucwinch&tabID=T001&docId=CB332 7675440&type=multipage&contentSet=ECCOArticles&version=1.0&doc Level=FASCIMILE.

ARTICLE IN A PRINT JOURNAL

Roche, E. (2010) 'Seven Handel Oratorios.' *Early Music* 38, pp.313–16.

ARTICLE IN AN ONLINE JOURNAL

Kankaraš, M. and Moors G. (2012) 'Cross-National and Cross-Ethnic Differences in Attitudes: A Case of Luxembourg.' *Cross-Cultural Research*, 46, pp.224–54. Accessed 31 August 2012. Available through: SAGE Journals.

ARTICLE IN A NEWSPAPER OR POPULAR MAGAZINE

Gibson, Owen. (2012) 'Paralympics 2012: gold for GB in velodrome and pool on first day.' *Guardian*, 31 August. 'The Olympic Games which have been neglected for such a length of time, seem to be again revived.' (1790). *The Times*, 6 September. [Accessed August 31, 2012]. http://infotrac.galegroup.com/itw/infomark/665/802/184711040w16/ purl=rc1_TTDA_0_CS51514150&dyn=3!xrn_1_0_ CS51514150&hst_1?sw_aep=ucwinch.

WEBSITE

A citation to website content can often be limited to a mention in the text or in a note ('As of August 29, 2012, Starbucks listed dairy and gluten free snacks on its website …'). If a more formal citation is desired, it may be styled as in the examples shown here. Because such content is subject to change, include an access date or, if available, a date that the site was last modified.

Starbucks. (2012) 'Chocolate Hazelnut Loaf.' [www] Available from: http://starbucks.co.uk/menu/food-list/muffins-pastries-and-doughnuts/ caramelised-hazelnut-and-belgian-chocolate-chunk-muffin. [Accessed August 29, 2012].

FILM

A citation to a film might be to the whole, or to a named scene, which can precede the citation in quotation marks.

Star Wars II: Attack of the Clones (2002) Film. Directed by George Lucas. Beverly Hills, CA: Twentieth Century Fox.

EXAMPLE OF AUTHOR–DATE NOTING

Notice that this type of citation requires a different writing style:

> This essay will argue that Handel's music evolved comprehensively while he was in London, following the changes in English musical fashion and due to the politics of English music performance. It will further argue that the product of his musical evolution—the English Oratorio—was successful because it appealed to the growing sense of religiously inspired English nationalism in the mid-eighteenth century. One of the most enduring myths about Handel's Messiah is that George II stood up during the first performance of the 'Hallelujah' chorus. His action (which has until recently been repeated at all performances of the oratorio) commanded his estranged son, Frederick Prince of Wales, with his cronies, who made up the opera party to stand also. As the film, The Great Mr Handel demonstrates (Walker, 1942), at a stroke Italian opera fell out of fashion and the English oratorio was born. Donald Burrows (2012) does much to dispel such nonsense. Instead, he suggests that Handel was a hardheaded businessman who found success with a more economically viable musical form. His biography argues that Handel took advantage of the financial collapse of Prince Frederick's Middlesex opera company, with its expensive productions and Italian prima donnas. In its stead, he put on a series of oratorio seasons, beginning in Lent 1743. These had the advantage of having no costumes, no sets, and, being sung in English, no Italian opera stars to pay. All this demonstrates a comprehensive evolution in Handel's music, but this essay must look elsewhere to find reasons whether and why Handel's musical evolution was successful in terms other than financial. The first source we shall turn to, Calvin Stapert (2010) argues that the Messiah in particular, and English oratorio in general, offered its audience 'exciting, entertaining stories in English about the heroes of a divinely favoured nation that was readily identified with England, and a composer with all the requisite skills to set those stories to music in a most compelling manner' (Stapert 2010, p.35). What is odd about Stapert's reading of the English oratorio, however, is that while he agrees that its appearance fitted the political context of music performance, and appealed to the growing sense of religiously inspired English nationalism in the mid-eighteenth century, he believes that Handel's music at this time was not the product of evolution. Instead, he argues that Handel presented the English audience with an English version

of a pre-existing tradition of Italian oratorio. A close examination of each of the arguments of Burrows and Stapert will demonstrate that a position somewhere between the two, which accepts Handel's musical evolution, but at the same time, which points to a growing sense of nationalism in England, gives the best answer to the question as to how far Handel's music evolved in London in the 1740s. It was comprehensive and successful. Evidence (Gilman 2009) will be presented to make this point clear. Gilman argues that Handel was not alone in altering his style of music to capture the growing fervour of nationalism in the mid-eighteenth century. Thomas Augustine Arne wrote the indelible favourite 'Rule Britannia!' (Arne 1742) to suit the same political climate and at the same time that Handel turned to writing English oratorio. But Arne was writing English opera for private performance for Frederick, Prince of Wales at his home at Cliveden, and his work has largely disappeared from the repertoire. On the other hand, Handel wrote English oratorio to help a wide theatre going-audience feel good about their country, and his oratorios are still regularly performed.

EXAMPLE OF AN AUTHOR–DATE CITATION LIST

Arne, T. A. and D. Mallett, 1742. *Alfred: an opera.* London: J. Walsh.

Burrows, D. 2012. *Handel: The Master Musicians*, 2nd edn. Oxford: Oxford University Press.

Gilman, T. (2009). 'Arne, Handel, the Beautiful, and the Sublime.' *Eighteenth-Century Studies* 42, pp.529–555.

The Great Mr Handel. (1942) Film. Directed by Norman Walker. London: G. H. W. Productions Ltd.

Stapert, C. 2010. *Handel's Messiah: Comfort for God's People.* Grand Rapids, Wm. B. Eerdmans.

Index